How to Read Music for Any Instrument

Daily Exercises to Understand Music in 21 Days

By: Barton Press

Table of Contents

Foreword

Welcome to this comprehensive guide about how to read and understand music! Perhaps you are here because you desire to start studying how to play an instrument or to get serious about singing. Whether you are starting as a total beginner or are a more seasoned musician looking to brush up on your musical knowledge, this guide covers every notational aspect of music on the page needed to understand music for any instrument.

Because music contains many facets that require in-depth explanation, this guide has been conceptually divided into three weeks, twenty-one days. Each week focuses on an overall topic broken down into seven days, and each day focuses on a subject to analyze and practice in an appropriate order. Exercises will be included daily to apply the given musical focus for that day, so knowledge can be applied and practiced as you gain it.

Listening examples are also included throughout to give reference to certain discussions. The suggested listening examples feature music from around the world in various styles and genres ranging from rock and pop to classical and jazz. Feel free to use your preferred listening platform, such as YouTube, Spotify, or Apple Music to search the suggested musical piece or song.

At the end of this guide you will find a glossary of terms and symbols for quick reference to all terminology and music notation you will encounter. Also, on day three, you will learn about durations of notes and rests. These notations have two different names for the same symbol in English, one in American English and one in British English. This guide will use the American English names; however, the British English equivalents are noted on the page upon which they occur, and are also included in the glossary at the end of the guide for reference. Let's get started!

Week 1 – Rhythm & Timing

The main objectives this first week will be understanding the complexities of timing and rhythm in music. Rhythm is closely related to math in how it combines and divides to create various durations of sounds and silence. Don't worry- even if math isn't your favorite academic subject, rhythm is simple math - no algebra or geometry here!

Before you begin exploring the first part of our day-by-day guide, here is some necessary information to keep in mind throughout the week. First, you will need access to a tool called a metronome. This is an essential device that will aid in accurately performing the daily exercises this week. This tool can be purchased as an electronic device from many music retailers, but you are not required to go out and spend money. Metronomes are also available online for free and as applications on any smartphone.

When practicing the daily exercises, an instrument will not be necessary. Your voice and hands will be sufficient to execute each exercise this week. It is crucial to repeat the given exercises until mastery is achieved before continuing to the next day of the guide. Studying timing and rhythm in music requires learning to count within the context of the music. You will see counts written in many of the exercises of each day to aid in understanding the relationships of notes and sequence. Verbally counting aloud is highly encouraged to audibly hear the duration and divisions of notes as they occur.

That being said, there are dozens of counting methods that may be used to teach yourself to read rhythm and feel timing. The counting system used in this guide is a number-based system that can be applied universally. Because the focus this week is solely on timing, the notation and symbols will be limited to rhythmic topics. The exercises featured will not be on a full music staff and are written on simplistic rhythm lines. Let's get started!

Day 1 - Pulse - Music's Heartbeat

Before studying how to read notes from the page, we need to first establish that music has a steady, nearly constant **pulse**. The pulse in music is quite like that of the human heartbeat. For both music and a heartbeat, the pulse should beat at a steady, consistent rate. Our heart may beat more quickly when we run or more slowly when we are at rest, however, once it settles into a pulse, a normal heartbeat keeps a steady pace. Similarly, music can also beat quickly or slowly.

The pulse in music cannot be seen with our eyes; it is heard with our ears and felt with our body. By tapping, clapping, drumming, or counting aloud, it is possible to create an audible pulse. The motion of foot-tapping or head bobbing to a catchy song is often synchronized to the sound and feeling of the pulse. The pulse is frequently referred to as the **beat** in music, so pulse and beat are often used interchangeably. For some beginning musicians, feeling the beat comes naturally, while some beginners may have to practice to develop a steady beat.

Composers (people who write music) use symbols to visually group the pulse into beats of sound and silence. To begin with, we are going to practice keeping a steady beat with these two symbols:

This is a quarter note and gets 1 beat of sound

This is a quarter rest and gets 1 beat of silence

Exercise 1.1

Try tapping, clapping, or saying "tah" to the line of quarter notes and quarter rests below. Think or say "rest" to help feel the beats of silence.

You may be uncertain of whether you stayed steady as you performed the exercise. Luckily, there is a device that aids the player in developing and assessing steadiness. A **metronome** is a tool that produces an audible sound, such as a click or beep, and ideally a synchronized visual motion component, like a pendulum or a blinking light. Tapping or clapping with the metronome will train the ears and body to hear and feel a steady pulse. They are available in multiple formats such as physical devices (purchasable online and at local music retailers), interactive online metronomes, and even as applications for smartphones.

Before beginning to practice with the metronome, the speed of the music will need to be determined. The speed of music is most commonly called the **tempo** and often indicated at the top of the music as the **tempo marking.** The user can set the tempo of the metronome using a number system called **Beats Per Minute**, or **BPM** for short. The speed of the click corresponds with how low or high the number. For example, 100 BPM would be twice as fast as 50 BPM, and 60 BPM would be the same speed as a ticking clock (60 seconds in a minute=60 BPM). If the tempo marking is indicated in BPM, it will often be notated with a quarter note, equal sign, and then the BPM number. For example, marking below would indicate to set the metronome to 60 BPM.

$$\quarternote = 60$$

The following beat exercises have tempo markings in BPM (Beats Per Minute). Before beginning each, set and start the metronome to the number indicated, and listen for a moment to internalize the tempo. Then begin tapping, clapping, or vocalizing where there are beats of sound, and thinking "rest" on the beats of silence.

Exercise 1.2

Exercises 1.3

Exercise 1.4

Day 2 - Meter & Musical Punctuation

So far, we've learned that music is organized into beats of sound and silence that follow a steady pulse. The exercises presented yesterday were simplistic beat exercises that intentionally omitted multiple facets of notation. Each line was like a paragraph with no punctuation, or a rough draft, but today we will punctuate our musical paragraph.

Here is Exercise 1.1 from Day 1 again, but with symbols added that assemble the music more cohesively (or punctuate it for clarity of organization). These symbols are circled to aid in identification.

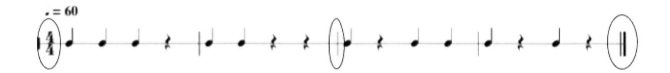

Let's examine the new symbols individually from left to right. At the beginning of the line, before any notes or rests, is the **time signature,** or **meter.** Meter is how music is sequenced into beats within bar lines and measures. The time signature is the printed notation of a specific meter, so time signature and meter are often used interchangeably. The time signature is written as a number stacked on top of another. The top number signifies how many beats per measure, and the bottom number tells what unit gets the beat. So, in the above example, the meter is four counts per measure with the quarter note receiving the beat. You can also think of this like a fraction with the 4 on the bottom being like a quarter (4 quarter beats per measure). For today, the time signatures studied will exclusively have four as the bottom number.

In the center, there is a single, thin vertical line called the **bar line**. This line divides the music into segments to create smaller, measurable groups of notes and rests. The space between each bar line is called a **measure,** which is a group of notes and rests that have a specific number of beats. It is also commonly called a **bar**. The line of music above has four measures/bars from beginning to end, with four total beats in each one.

On the far right there are two, short, vertical lines, one thick and one thin. This is called the **double bar line**, and it simply indicates that the song, musical excerpt, or exercise has ended.

The time signature, measures, notes and rests will direct us in how to count and feel the rhythm of music. **Rhythm** is defined as the systematic arrangement of musical sounds, principally according to duration and periodic stress. Rhythm in music is characterized by the repeating sequence of stressed and unstressed beats occurring within a measure. A beat with stress is called a **strong beat** and is felt with slight emphasis in comparison to an unstressed, or **weak beat**.

C   This symbol is an additional way to notate 4/4 time signature. Because 4/4 is the most common meter used in music, the "c" abbreviates "**common time**".

2/4   The two on top in this meter indicates two beats per measure. The four on the bottom continues to indicate that the quarter note receives the beat.

3/4   The three on top in this meter indicates three beats per measure. The four on the bottom continues to indicate that the quarter note receives the beat.

These are the most commonly found time signatures in music. Additional time signatures will be discussed later in the guide.

The **downbeat** is always the first beat of a measure, and it is the most emphasized strong beat in any time signature. Music continuously leads forward to the downbeat of the next measure. The final beat of a measure is called the **upbeat,** because it precedes and anticipates the subsequent downbeat. The downbeat will always be beat one, however the upbeat will vary depending on the time signature. In 4/4, the upbeat is beat four, but in 3/4, it is beat three. In 2/4, every measure is solely a downbeat and an upbeat, because beat one is the downbeat and beat two is the upbeat.

The relationship of strong and weak beats is best demonstrated by listening to examples of music in various meters. For each time signature, a variety of listening suggestions will be mentioned. When listening, listen for the beat and see if you can distinguish the first beat of each measure.

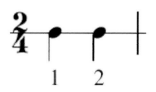

In 2/4 time, beat 1 of each measure is considered the strong beat, and beat 2 of each measure is considered the weak beat. This typically gives music in 2/4 the feel of a march, and 2/4 meter is commonly used for polkas, galops, and marches.

Suggested listening for 2/4 time:

March - "The Stars and Stripes Forever" by John Philip Sousa
Galop – "The Can-Can" by Jacques Offenbach
Polka – "Hoop Dee Doo Polka by "Frankie Yankovic"

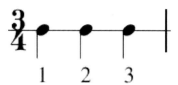

In 3/4 time, beat 1 is also considered the strong beat, and beat 2 and 3 are felt as weak beats. 3/4 is often used for waltzes and minuets.

Suggested listening for 3/4 time:

Waltz – "The Blue Danube Waltz" by Johann Strauss
Minuet – "Minuet in G Major" by Johann Sebastian Bach
Popular – "My Favorite Things" from *The Sound of Music*

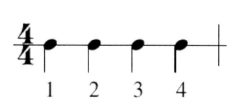

In 4/4 time, beat 1 is the strong beat with beat 3 as a secondary strong beat. Beat 2 and 4 are considered the weak beats. 4/4 is referred to as *common time* because it is the most used time signature in multiple genres of music.

Suggested listening for 4/4 time:

Ragtime – "The Entertainer" by Scott Joplin
Classical – "Ode to Joy" by Ludwig Van Beethoven
Rock – "Yellow Submarine" by The Beatles

As we learn to count rhythms, the time signature determines how the counts will be sequenced. It is helpful to both write in the counts for each measure and say them aloud while tapping/clapping. The following exercises feature a suggested way to write in the counts. Notice that the beats of rests are in parenthesis to represent a counted beat of silence.

Get into the habit of checking the time signature before you begin. Also, it is helpful to count aloud a full, "free" measure before beginning each line. Feel free to set your metronome anywhere between 60-100BPM. Repeat each at several tempos for a challenge!

Exercise 2.1

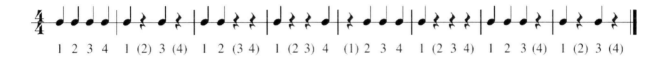

1 2 3 4   1 (2) 3 (4)   1 2 (3 4)   1 (2 3) 4   (1) 2 3 4   1 (2 3 4)   1 2 3 (4)   1 (2) 3 (4)

Exercise 2.2

1   2   1   2   1   2   1   (2)   1   (2)   1   (2)   (1)   2   1   (2)

Exercise 2.3

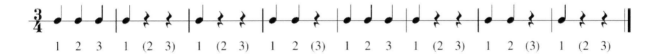

1   2   3   1   (2   3)   1   (2   3)   1   2   (3)   1   2   3   1   (2   3)   1   2   (3)   1   (2   3)

The final punctuation to discuss today is the **repeat sign.** Recall that a double-bar line is placed at the end of a piece to signify the end. However, if at the end there is a double-bar line with two dots, it symbolizes the piece has not yet ended. Those dots change the meaning of the double-bar line and create a repeat sign. A repeat sign stipulates to play the music once again or repeat it.

Exercise 2.4 below features a repeat sign at the end of the line. This type of repeat sign indicates that once the end of the line is reached, start again from the very beginning. The repeat sign is circled for clarity. Practice tapping or clapping the line below with the repeat sign. Try to be precise in keeping a steady pulse. The upbeat of the final measure should lead into the downbeat of the first measure when repeating the line. Use the metronome to help measure your steadiness. The objective is to not miss a beat, so look ahead to prepare for the jump back to the beginning.

Exercise 2.4

Repeat signs can also be paired to create shorter repeated sections. In these instances, the signs will face each other, as notated in the example below. In the Exercise 2.5, the paired repeat signs indicate to only repeat the last two measures of the line. So, start from the beginning and play to the end, and then also play the last two measures once again to complete the exercise.

Exercise 2.5

The last type of repeat sign is similar to the previous one. The repeat signs are paired again, but there are two segments of repeated music. To complete this line, play the first five measures twice, and then the last four measures twice.

Exercise 2.6

Meter and counting will continue to be prevalent as we continue our journey this week. "Musical Punctuation" and counting are essential to every type of music we'll ever encounter, so be sure you have a strong grasp of today's concepts before continuing to Day 3.

Day 3 - Duration & Counting - Musical Math

Today, we will explore symbols that expand upon how durations of sound are notated beyond a single beat. Collectively, these symbols will be referred to as **durations** because each symbol represents how many beats a sound or silence should be sustained for or held.

The duration of any sound or rest is conceptualized by the notational facets of each symbol. The ovalish dot part of each note is called the **note head**. The vertical line coming from some of the note heads is called a **stem**. When studying rhythmic values and their names, take note of the differences in their appearance. Notice if the note head is solid or open, and whether or not there is a stem.

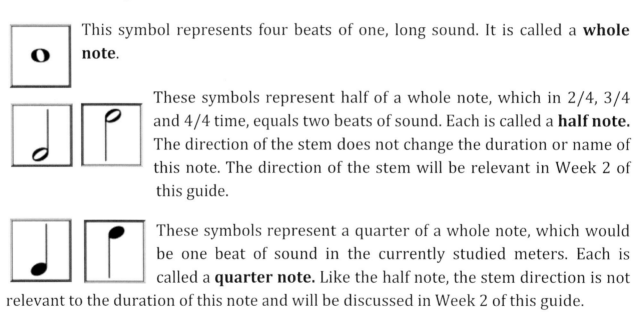

This symbol represents four beats of one, long sound. It is called a **whole note**.

These symbols represent half of a whole note, which in 2/4, 3/4 and 4/4 time, equals two beats of sound. Each is called a **half note**. The direction of the stem does not change the duration or name of this note. The direction of the stem will be relevant in Week 2 of this guide.

These symbols represent a quarter of a whole note, which would be one beat of sound in the currently studied meters. Each is called a **quarter note.** Like the half note, the stem direction is not relevant to the duration of this note and will be discussed in Week 2 of this guide.

Because a whole note is a single note that is played for the duration of four beats, it is difficult to implement with tapping or clapping since those are shorter sounds. However, speaking, singing, or playing a sound on an instrument will demonstrate the whole note more effectively. Try humming and holding the hum sound for four beats. Now try humming for two beats, and then one beat to also practice half note and quarter note this way. When practicing while counting aloud, longer durations such as the whole note can also be shown by keeping your hands clasped together for the entire duration to demonstrate the holding of the note and bouncing them on each beat.

Try the aforementioned humming and counting techniques when practicing Exercise 3.1. Durations of more than one count are notated with underlines beneath the counts to demonstrate how those counts are grouped and belong to the note printed above them. Also, notice that when a half note appears on the second half of the measure, it starts on beat three and takes the duration of both beats three and four in the measure, which is still two counts worth. Remember to check the time signature, look for repeat signs, and count in your head as you hum along.

Exercise 3.1

1 2 3 4   1~2 3~4   1~2 3~4   1~2~3~4   1~2~3~4   1~2 3~4   1~2 3~4   1 2 3 4

The notes pictured above are all durations of sound. Each symbol has a corresponding symbol that represents durations of silence. These durations of silence, called **rests**, have equivalent names to reflect their respective durations.

 This first symbol represents a whole measure of rest. Most often, this holds for four beats because most music is in 4/4 time. A **whole rest** can be used as a three-beat rest in 3/4 time, however, in this case it is interpreted to be "rest for the entire measure." Notice how it hangs below the line because it is heavy and covers the "whole" measure.

 A **half rest** is two beats of silence in most meters. Its appearance is like the whole rest. To distinguish the two, the whole rest sits below the line, and the half rest sits above, like a tophat on a head.

 A **quarter rest** is one beat of silence in the currently studied meters.

Hum, sing, clap, or tap the following exercises incorporating the new rests learned. Parentheses are placed around counts that occur on the rest which aids in counting the duration of each rest. It may be helpful to whisper the counts in parentheses on the rest to maintain steadiness of pulse. Always check the time signature and use a metronome.

Exercise 3.2

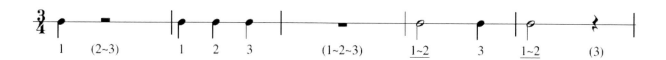

Exercise 3.3

Take note of the whole rest in each of the previous exercises. In the 4/4 line, the whole rest is found in the sixth measure. It is found in the third measure of the 3/4 line. Although the symbol is the exact same, they are not the same duration of counts. Because a whole rest represents a "whole measure of rest", its duration depends on the time signature in which it is found. In 4/4, it receives four beats of silence, but in 3/4 it receives three beats of silence as shown with the counts in parentheses below those measures. However, a whole note cannot be used in 3/4 time.

The rhythmic values we've discussed so far have been whole numbers due to the above notes and rests being single to multiple beats of duration. Music starts to get even more interesting when we divide a single beat into smaller durations. This creates multiple sounds within a single beat, which offers opportunities for faster rhythms.

The following are divisions of a single beat. Observe the appearance of each note in relation to the note heads, stems, and additional markings referred to as the hook or flag.

  These are called **eighth notes**, and they are worth an eighth of a whole note. This would be half of a beat in the currently studied meters. They have a solid note head, a stem, and one **hook/flag**.

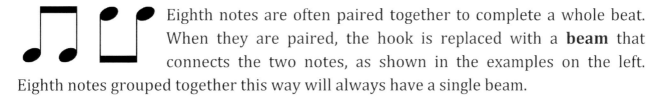 Eighth notes are often paired together to complete a whole beat. When they are paired, the hook is replaced with a **beam** that connects the two notes, as shown in the examples on the left. Eighth notes grouped together this way will always have a single beam.

Groups of multiple eighth notes beyond two can also be beamed together in a similar fashion. It is quite common to see four eighth notes beamed together over two beats. As long as it is a single beam, this does not change the duration at all. The eighth notes would be performed exactly the same as if they were beamed by twos.

Learning to count eighth notes is best approached by establishing the concept of dividing the beat. Two eighth notes occupy a single beat and divide it into two separate sounds. In 4/4 time, dividing all of the beats can be counted as "1-and-2-and-3-and-4-and", and is more simply written "1+2+3+4+" (the word "and" will be abbreviated as "+" and not read as plus). The "and" or "+" between each beat is the division of the beat. Hearing and feeling this division are vital to properly performing eighth notes. Try tapping a steady beat with your hand or foot. The beats, "1-2-3-4", occur when the foot or hand comes down, while the "ands" occur when the hand or foot is up. This demonstrates the feeling of dividing the beat.

In Exercise 3.4, counts are written below each note including the new eighth note divisions. Try saying the counts aloud with a steady pulse to feel the speed of the eighth note. The eighth notes should sound evenly split within the beat. Repeat as needed with a metronome to get the division in the second measure precise.

Exercise 3.4

An eighth note can be divided to create a subdivision of the beat called a **sixteenth note**. Pictured below are various forms of sixteenth notes. A single sixteenth note is 1/16 of a whole note. This is 1/4 of a single beat in the currently studied meters. Sixteenth notes have a solid note head, a stem, and two hooks/flags or beams, and, like eighth notes, they are often grouped together. Most commonly, sixteenth notes are grouped into fours, since this would complete one beat in our current time signatures, but they can also be grouped into twos or threes. There must be two flags/hooks or beams to distinguish them from the single hook/beam of eighth notes.

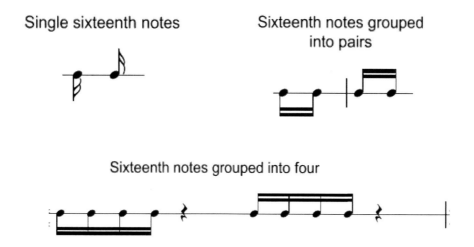

To count sixteenth notes, the beat must be subdivided into four parts. Since there would be four separate sounds within a beat, four syllables are used to audibly subdivide the beat. The first sound is the number of the beat, i.e. "1". The second subdivision is commonly the letter "e", the third is "+", which is still read as "and", and the fourth and final subdivision is the letter "a", which is pronounced as "ah". A group of four sixteenth notes in 4/4 time would count as 1e+a, or 2e+a, or 3e+a, or 4e+a depending on what beat of the measure the grouping were to occur. When saying and feeling the counts, all four sounds need to be evenly split and timed within the beat the notes belong.

In Exercise 3.5 below, the sixteenth notes are beamed into a group of four, thus occupying one full beat of duration. Turn on your metronome to 60 BPM and say the

16

counts aloud for this exercise. Then clap/tap/sing at the same speed to harness the subdivision of the sixteenth notes.

Exercise 3.5

This diagram below offers a clear representation of how note durations relate and divide. Use this as a quick reference for counting and learning the relationships between all of the notes discussed.

Rhythm Tree

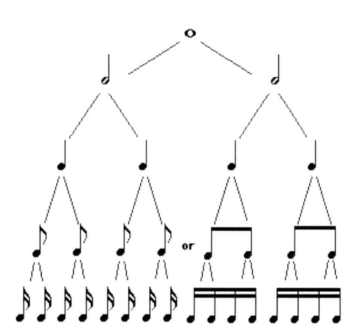

There are several ways eighth notes, and sixteenth notes can be combined within a single beat. To start, we will examine the two most common. One eighth note followed by two sixteenth notes equals one beat. This would be counted as 1e+a. The second subdivision of the beat, (e), is felt but not played, since the eighth note encompasses both the first and second subdivision of the beat. Two sixteenth notes followed by one eighth notes equals one beat, and would be counted 1e+a. In this rhythmic sequence, the fourth subdivision of the beat is felt but not played, because the eighth note starts on the "+" and (a) is included in the eighth note's duration.

In the first measure of exercise 3.6, the eighth note is first, then followed by a pair of sixteenth notes. The counts are written accordingly, with the first group occurring on beat one, and the second on beat two. Stem direction is flipped for comparison, but does not change the counts or durations of the notes. The second measure presents the reverse — the sixteenth note pair is first followed by the eighth note, and the counts are written according. Set your metronome to 50-60BPM and try saying these counts aloud. The goal is to have each figure occur within one beat.

Exercise 3.6

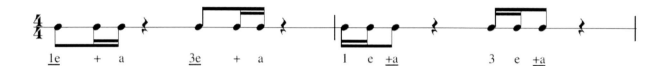

1e   +   a   3e   +   a   1   e   +a   3   e   +a

Suggested listening for eighth-sixteenth-sixteenth rhythm:

Opera – "William Tell Overture" by Gioachino Rossini

Suggested listening for sixteenth-sixteenth-eighth rhythm:

Pop – "Attention" by Charlie Puth

Like with the notes and rests previously studied in day two, eighth notes and sixteenth notes have corresponding rests of the same duration pictured below.

 An **eighth rest** has one flag or hook to represent its relationship to the eighth note. Its silent duration is the same as an eighth note, which is 1/8 of a whole note.

 A **sixteenth rest** has two flags or hooks to represent its relationship to the sixteenth note. It is silent for the duration of a sixteenth note, which is 1/16 of a whole note.

The following exercises feature the note and rest values studied today. The counts are included in Exercises 3.7 and 3.8 to aid in comprehension.

Exercise 3.7

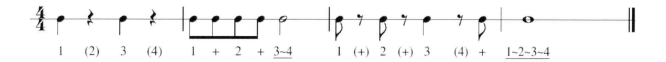

Exercise   **3.8**

Copy the last two exercises below onto a sheet of paper and write the counts below each note/measure. Refer to the content studied today for assistance, and check the time signature, then confirm the accuracy of your written counts with the answer key found on page 138 of the guide. Next practice humming or singing each line. Remember to use a metronome set at a slow BPM such as 60 to keep steady and divide and subdivide eighth and sixteenth notes evenly.

Exercise 3.9

Exercise 3.10

Day 4 - Dots, Ties, & Pick-Up Notes

In our studies so far, there have been 1/4, 1/2, 1, 2, and 4 beat durations. By adding a few simple markings, these durations can be augmented to include all durations between and beyond. The first to discuss is the musical **tie**.

When a curved line *connects* two notes of the same pitch, it combines these note values into one, longer value. Rather than sounding two separate notes, the duration of the first is extended to include the note to which the first is tied. Basically, the duration of the tied notes is the sum of their values.

In the image above, there is a whole note tied to a whole note. Rather than sounding two separate four-count whole notes, this would become a longer sound of eight beats of duration. Any combination of rhythms can be tied together to create additional durations, like the quarter notes below.

Two quarter notes tied together would be worth two counts. This commonly occurs when the composer wishes to have two beats occur "over the bar line". This expression refers to the last and first beat of the measure being tied together, as is shown in the example of tied quarter notes above.

The exercises on the next page contain additional examples of tied notes. Notice that the tie can be found above or below the notes. It will usually be on the opposite side of the stems for clarity in notation. Rests are never tied together, and multiple notes can be tied together as long as a different duration cannot be substituted. For example, you would not see four quarter notes tied together in a single measure of 4/4, because a whole note would be used instead.

Practice the following exercises incorporating ties in multiple time signatures. The counts encompassed within the tied durations are underlined to assist. Use a metronome set to a slow BPM such as 60, check the time signature, and keep steady as you hum, tap, or clap along.

Exercise 4.1

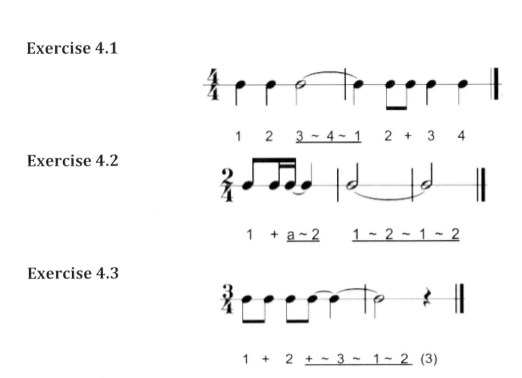

Exercise 4.2

Exercise 4.3

Let's say a composer wants to write a rhythm that lasts three counts. Theoretically, a half note tied to a quarter note would equal three counts, however this is not the proper way to notate a three-beat duration. This is where the **rhythmic dot** comes into play. If a small, single dot follows the note head of any given note, it adds half of the value of the note to which it is attached. So, instead of tying a half note to a quarter note to achieve a three-beat note, a half note with a dot is used instead. This symbol is officially named a **dotted-half note,** and it has a value of three beats.

Dotted-half notes are common in 3/4 and 4/4 meter, and particularly useful in 3/4 for having a full-measure-note duration. The dot will always follow the given notes, whether stem up or down. It cannot be used in 2/4 meter because it is too long of a duration for a two-count measure.

Below are rhythm lines containing dotted half notes. Copy the lines onto a sheet of paper and write in the counts. Consult the answer key on page 138 to ensure accuracy of your written counts. Consult the time signature and use underlines to indicate longer durations. The dotted half note will receive three total counts. Then, hum the lines that incorporate the new dotted half note. Always use a metronome to maintain steadiness.

Exercise 4.4

Exercise 4.5

It is important to clarify that the dot doesn't necessarily add one beat to any note. This is only the case for a dotted half note. The type of note the dot is attached to determines the duration the dot adds. When attached to a half note, which is two counts, the dot itself is then one beat, since half of two is one. Study the following musical equations for a visual representation of the duration of the dot.

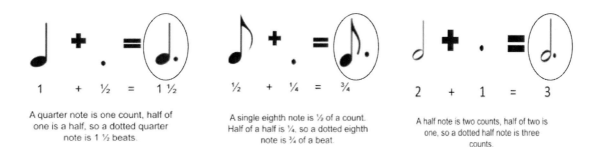

A quarter note is one count, half of one is a half, so a dotted quarter note is 1 ½ beats.

A single eighth note is ½ of a count. Half of a half is ¼, so a dotted eighth note is ¾ of a beat.

A half note is two counts, half of two is one, so a dotted half note is three counts.

On the far left is a dotted quarter note equation. Because a quarter note is one count (in most time signatures), the dot adds a half of a beat of duration. A dotted quarter is one and a half beats total. In the middle equation, the dot gets 1/4 of a beat because half of an eighth note is 1/4. Therefore, a dotted eighth note is 3/4 of a beat. The last equation is the dotted half note worth three beats.

Let's explore these dotted rhythms in context of rhythmic sequences in music. Since a dotted half note is a full number value, three, it can stand alone because it completes three beats. A dotted half note would be full measure in 3/4 time, and in 4/4 it might be paired with notes or rests occupying one beat of duration. A dotted quarter note, however, will nearly always be found paired with an eighth note, because together, they complete two beats. This is because a dotted quarter is worth an uneven duration, one and a half beats.

To assist in counting rhythms like this, it is helpful to divide the beat. This means feeling the counts on the beat and between the beats (i.e. 1-and-2-and-3-and-4-and, or 1+2+3+4+). Counting the "ands" or division of the beat is essential to count off beat rhythms like a dotted quarter note paired with an eighth note, because the eighth note will happen between the beats.

For example, in the next example, the dotted quarter note takes counts 1+2, and the single eighth note occurs on the + of beat 2. This means the eighth note is on the off-beat, or the second division of beat two.

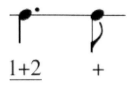

1+2   +

Another helpful visual to aid understanding the dotted quarter note is to temporarily divide the dotted quarter note into eighth notes. This aids in feeling all three divisions (1-and-2) so that the eighth note following the dotted/tied rhythm (+) is properly placed in time. In practice, the rhythm sequences directly above and directly below are counted and sound the same.

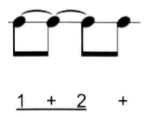

1   +   2   +

The final dotted rhythm duration to study in this guide is the dotted eighth note. Because it is 3/4 of a full beat, it is often paired with a single sixteenth note, and they are most often beamed together to neatly group into a complete beat. In the example below, the dotted-eighth-note-sixteenth rhythm occurs on beat two of the measure. First, we subdivide the second beat into sixteenth notes, 2e+a. Then group the "2e+" with the dotted eighth note, as shown with the underline. The sixteenth note receives the subdivision "a" at the end of the beat.

1 e + a 2 e+ a

When beamed together, the eighth note and sixteenth note share a full beam. The sixteenth note also has a partial beam facing toward the eighth note, or inward.

Let's also temporarily divide the dotted eighth note into three tied sixteenth notes for a visual conceptualization of the subdivision of the dotted eighth note. These two rhythms would sound exactly the same. The first is the common notation, and the second clarifies how to subdivide and count this complex rhythm.

For both the dotted quarter note and dotted eight notes rhythms, the pairings can be reversed to have the dotted note follow its partnered note. The duration and amount of counts remains the same, but the counts themselves will vary depending on what beat the rhythm occurs and which rhythm is first.

All rhythmic sequences require familiarity practice to perform accurately. Here are a few iconic listening examples that frequently use dotted rhythms.

Suggested listening for Dotted quarter note-eighth rhythm:

Traditional lullaby - "All Through the Night" by Edward Jones

Suggested listening for Dotted eighth note-sixteenth rhythm:

March - "Battle Hymn of the Republic" by William Steffe

Now that the time signatures, measures, and note durations are established, we can discuss the **anacrusis**. Sometimes in music, there will be a note or sequence of notes that occur before the first complete measure/bar of a piece. This is an incomplete measure in any given time signature, and "picks-up" into the first measure. This is more often called a **pick-up note** due to the nature of it "picking up" into the first full measure of the music. The terms pick-up note, anacrusis, and upbeat are often used synonymously.

If a piece of music has a pick-up note, the final measure of that piece should be shortened that number of beats so that the anacrusis and the last measure complete a full measure. Analyze exercise 4.6 below. Because the time signature is 3/4, the anacrusis at the very beginning occurs on beat three. Notice that the final measure is only two counts to account for the one beat pick-up. Together, they complete three counts for a complete measure in 3/4.

Exercise 4.6

Perform this exercise using a metronome.

Pick-up notes may use various rhythms, so an eighth or sixteenth note can also be an anacrusis. If the anacrusis is less than a beat, it is a partial-beat pick-up and will occur on the division or subdivision of the beat as if it were whole.

Exercise 4.7

When rehearsing exercise 4.7, count a "free" bar before beginning. Think "(1-2-3-4) and" to place the pick-up eighth note accurately. Counts are included for clarity. In some music, the initial rest may be omitted.

Multiple notes can be used as an anacrusis as well. In this situation, first determine the number of beats in the incomplete anacrusis measure if more than one. If there are three beats at the beginning but the time signature is 4/4, then the pick-up would count 2 - 3 - 4, as demonstrated in exercise 4.8 below. Notice that the last measure is a single beat to account for the first incomplete measure of three beats. Together, the anacrusis and final measure complete a full measure in the 4/4 time signature.

Exercise 4.8

For this exercise, count "(1-2-3-4-1) 2-3-4" to establish tempo before beginning.

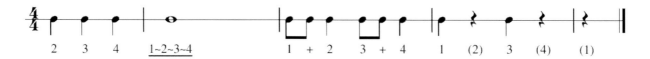

When beginning a musical piece that features any anacrusis, count a full bar in the given time signature before starting. Treat it as if there are imaginary rests before the pick-up note(s) in order to establish the beat, tempo, division (eight notes), subdivision (sixteenth notes), and counts to have a precise entrance.

Analyze and practice the following exercises incorporating dots, ties, and pick-up notes. Remember to check the time signature, count carefully, and use a metronome set at a slow BPM to start (BPM around 50-60). When preparing for a pick-up note or notes, count the beats in the bar leading up to the entrance.

Exercise 4.9

Exercise 4.10

Exercise 4.11

Day 5 - Simple vs. Compound Meter

To achieve a thorough understanding of rhythm and timing this week, many topics will be elaborated upon. On Day 2, we studied meter in music within three selected time signatures, 2/4, 3/4, and 4/4. To review, the top number of a time signature indicates the number of beats per measure/bar. The bottom number indicates what rhythmic value the beat receives. So far, only a four has been seen as the bottom number, so the quarter note received the beat. All of these are considered to be **simple meters,** these three time signatures divide the beat into two notes or sounds.

A time signature in a simple meter will always have a two, three, or four as the top number, and are classified as **duple, triple, or quadruple meter** accordingly. This is determined by the number of beats in each measure. For example, a two on the top of a time signature means it is duple, three is triple, and four is quadruple. 2/4 is considered a duple meter, 3/4 is a triple meter, and 4/4 is a quadruple meter, due to the number of beats in a measure determined by each top number.

Any given meter is considered simple if each beat divides into two notes or sounds. This is true of the meters we've studied thus far, because a quarter note represents one beat, and each quarter divides into two equal parts called eighth notes. The bottom number is not always four, however. If there is a two as the lower number, the half note receives one beat. If there is a 4 on the bottom, the quarter note receives one beat. And if there is an eight on the bottom, the eighth note receives one beat. There are multiple combinations of top and bottom numbers possible to create a meter. Let's begin with the various simple meter combinations.

Simple duple meter is any meter in which the beats are grouped into two (duple) within a measure, and the beat can be divided into two sounds (simple). 2/4 is a simple duple meter because there are two beats per measure (duple), and the beat (quarter note in this meter) divides into two notes/sounds (eighth notes). All simple duple meters will have a two as the top number.

2/2 is another example of a simple duple meter. The top number once again determines two beats per measure, however the bottom number stipulates that the half note receives the beat this time, rather than the quarter note like in 2/4. The half note gets one count in 2/2, so there can be two half notes per measure. Quarter notes are counted using the division (1+2+), and eighth notes are counted using the subdivision (1e+a, 2e+a).

Exercise 5.1

This exercise is in 2/2 meter with counts included to put this into context. This changes our previously discussed durations of counting. After analyzing this, rehearse this exercise with a metronome using the counts printed for guidance in this new time signature.

2/2 is often also referred to as **cut-time**, which is notated as a "C" with a vertical line through it, as pictured to the left. The cut-time symbol was inspired by the symbol for common time mentioned in Day 3. Common time is equal to 4/4, and cut-time is equal to 2/2. Music written in a march style frequently uses cut-time as the meter.

Theoretically, 2/8 would be another simple duple meter, however it is not commonly used. Once again, the top number is a two (duple), but now the bottom number is an eight. This indicates that the eighth note receives the beat, and the beat would divide into two sixteenth notes.

Simple triple meter is any meter in which the beats are grouped into three per measure, with the beat divisible into two. There will always be a three on the top in any simple triple time signature. 3/4 is the most common, however 3/2 and 3/8 are also found in music.

The two on the bottom of this time signature indicates the half note receives the beat, like 2/2 or cut-time. The difference is that there is an additional beat in each measure.

The eight on the bottom of this time signature indicates the eighth note receives the beat, like in 2/8. Here, the difference is the additional beat per measure because the top number is 3 (triple), rather than 2 (duple).

The final simple meter to examine is the **simple quadruple meter.** For a time signature to be a simple quadruple meter, it must have four beats per measure, with each beat divisible into two parts. 4/4 is a simple quadruple meter because there are four beats per measure, and the beat is divisible into two parts. Additional simple quadruple meters used are 4/2 and 4/8. The concepts mentioned previously with simple duple and simple triple meters apply here as well. When the lower number is two, the half note gets the beat, and when the lower number is eight, the eighth note gets the beat. Both 4/2 and 4/8 have four beats per measure (quadruple), but in the former the half receives one beat and, in the latter, the eighth note receives one beat.

The application of compound meters expands our time signature capabilities even further. In compound meters, the beat can be divided into three parts. This offers more complex time signatures. Let's start by examining 6/8, a **compound duple meter**. The purpose of the top and bottom numbers remains consistent across all meters, so in 6/8 there are six beats per measure and the eighth note gets one beat. Because it is a compound meter however, the division of the beat works differently. For simplicity, the six beats are going to be called "little beats", and these "little beats" can be grouped together to create two "big beats" in each measure (duple). The big beat would be a dotted quarter note, which can be divided into three eighth notes. This is what makes the meter compound; the main beat is a dotted quarter note, and it is divisible into three equal parts.

Exercise 5.2

This exercise contains common rhythmic combinations in 6/8. Initially, isolate each measure individually and rehearse it before stringing them together into a complete line. For your metronome setting, set the BPM to between 50-60 and use the tick for each individual "little" count. There will be six "ticks" (little beats) per measure.

An additional dotted quarter note beat can be added to each measure to create more compound meters. 9/8 has three main beats, each divisible into three parts, creating nine eighth-note divisions. 12/8 has four main beats, each also divisible into three parts, and would create twelve eighth-note divisions. The strong beats are felt at the beginning of every three note grouping. For example, in 6/8, the eighth-note division would be counted 1-2-3-4-5-6, with emphasis on beats 1 and 4. These are the strong beats in this meter, and are felt as if there are two beats per measure, making 6/8 duple meter. In 9/8, the count breakdown would be 1-2-3-4-5-6-7-8-9, and eighth note on beats 1, 4, and 7 would be the strong beats, creating a triple-beat feel per measure, thus a **compound triple meter**. And in 12/8, counted 1-2-3-4-5-6-7-8-9-10-11-12, emphasis would be placed on eighth notes 1, 4, 7, and 10 creating a **compound quadruple meter.**

Set your metronome to 50-60 BPM and rehearse exercises 5.3 and 5.4 below. Counts are included to assist with the new compound time signatures.

Exercise 5.3

Exercise 5.4

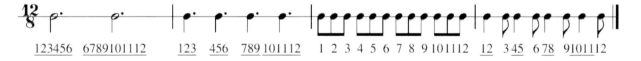

In each compound meter, the eighth notes can be subdivided into sixteenth notes. Because eighth notes are grouped into three to a beat, there can be six sixteenth notes to a beat. Each eighth note divides into two sixteenths, and with the eighth note receiving a count, the sixteenth notes are treated like a division is in simple meter. A full measure of sixteenth notes in 6/8 time would be counted 1+2+3+4+5+6+ as seen in Exercise 5.5.

Exercises 5.5

Set your metronome to 50-60 BPM. This time, there will be two sounds per beat because we are subdividing the eighth notes into two separate sounds. This will feel similar to eighth notes in simple time.

There are various ways to combine dotted quarter notes, quarter notes, eighth notes, sixteenth notes, and their corresponding rests in the compound meter. Use the division of the eighth note to assist in deciphering rhythms in 6/8, 9/8, or 12/8, and keep in mind that the eighth note technically receives one beat. A dotted quarter note equals three counts, a quarter note equals two counts, an eighth note equals one count, and a sixteenth note equals half of a count. Sixteenth notes will often be paired together to complete a whole beat. Quarter rests will also be found with a dot to occupy the same duration of a dotted quarter note in these meters.

Study and practice the following rhythm examples in compound meter to gain a thorough understanding of the various rhythmic combinations and sequences possible, setting the metronome to any BPM between 60-80.

Exercise 5.6

Exercise 5.7

When counting in compound meters, it is advisable to use the "little beat" to decipher the rhythm as we do in our approach above. Once accurate counting is established, we then examine the tempo of the music. The tempo ultimately determines whether to feel the main beat (dotted quarter note) or the eighth-note division while counting. Slower tempos are better felt with the eighth-note division, while faster tempos are better felt with the main beat. Sometimes, the tempo marking will even be marked to show which note duration to use as the beat. For example, if the tempo marking is set to the dotted quarter note, then the music is fast and it is best to follow the main beat, feeling a duple beat in 6/8, triple in 9/8, and quadruple in 12/8. If the tempo marking is set to the eighth note however, then the music is slower and the eighth note division should be followed. The examples below demonstrate the two ways a tempo marking may appear in music with compound meter.

$\quad \text{♩.} = \mathbf{96} \qquad\qquad\qquad \text{♪} = \mathbf{60}$

Suggested Listening for Fast Compound Meter:

Rock – "House of the Rising Sun" by the Animals
Irish Jig – "The Mist Covered Mountain" - Traditional

Suggested Listening for Slow Compound Meter:

Irish Ballad – "Red is the Rose" – Traditional
Baroque – "Jesu, Joy of Man's Desiring" by J. S. Bach

The time signatures and meters discussed above are the most frequently heard, seen, and used in music. As a beginning to late intermediate musician and/or reader of music, the music you are playing, singing, or reading won't extend beyond today's content. It should be noted, however, that musical meter is not restricted to the time signatures analyzed today. Uncommon and irregular meters are a deeper discussion reserved for a more advanced study of music theory.

On the next day of this week, the focus is a complex rhythmic sequence that requires prerequisite knowledge of eighth-note divisions and sixteenth-note subdivisions. Before beginning Day 6, return to Day 3 to review rhythm durations and counting to prepare for these challenging rhythms. The Rhythm Tree on page 19 offers a quick visual of how rhythmic durations combine and divide to aid in deciphering tomorrow's content.

Day 6 – Syncopation

The rhythm exercises practiced and studied thus far in our guide have been written with functional strong- and weak-beat relationships. Stressed and unstressed note values have been placed appropriately within the bar and given the music a sense of predictability and stability. For the most part, divided notes have occurred evenly contained within a beat and the music has felt balanced. Today, our examination of rhythm and timing is going to cover occurrences and combinations of rhythms that create an exciting, unpredictable feeling phenomenon.

When rhythm in music emphasizes unexpected parts of a measure, it is called **syncopation**. Syncopation is a temporary displacement of the strong versus weak beat structure in a measure. This displacement causes an unexpected interruption in the anticipated flow of the music. Syncopation is written in many forms and can be found in any meter. It is created by sequencing notes so that a sound occurs directly on the offbeat, division, or subdivision of the beat, usually resulting in stressing a weak beat of the measure. This allows for the music to become spontaneous, less predictable, and adds interest for the listener. It basically plays around with the beat of the music.

In its simplest form, syncopation can be created by replacing a strong beat with a rest. Take a measure of quarter notes in 4/4, for example. Usually, the downbeat (beat one) is the strongest, and the third beat is considered a secondary strong beat. Beats two and four would be considered the weak beats in relation. If either beat one or three were to be written as rests rather than notes, **even-beat syncopation** would occur. The weak beats of the measure would be emphasized due to there being a rest on the typically strong beat. Even-beat syncopation is most often used to create a **backbeat**. If the composer or songwriter wished, they could write a rest in place of both strong beats (one and three) and create what is referred to as a backbeat feel. This emphasizes only weak beats of the measure (two and four) and totally disrupts the usual strong beat pattern. Backbeat writing is common in pop, rock, and electronic music.

Suggested listening for backbeat feel:

Musical Theater – "Footloose", from the musical, *Footloose* by Tom Snow

A second way for syncopation to occur uses ties. To review, ties combine notes to create longer durations. Strong beats can be masked with ties by tying the final note, or upbeat, of a measure to the first note, or downbeat of the following measure. The downbeat still exists, but it isn't felt or distinctly heard due to the tie over the bar line, causing emphasis on the subsequent weak beats. A tie or half note could also mask the secondary strong beat in a 4/4 measure by tying beats two and three together, masking beat three and displacing the emphasis to beat four.

Exercise 6.1

Rehearse Exercise 6.1 using a metronome. Notice the underlined durations to account for the tie and half notes.

Syncopation can occur with divisions of the beat as well. A common syncopation rhythm heard in music is the eighth-quarter-eighth sequence. If occurring on beat one of a measure, this rhythm is counted as 1 +2 +. The first eighth note receives half of beat one, the quarter note receives the other half of beat one and half of beat two, and the last eighth note receives the other half of beat two.

Exercise 6.2

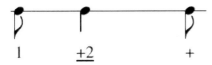

For exercise 6.2, set your metronome to 50-60 BPM and repeat the syncopated rhythm until mastery is achieved. Before beginning, say a full measure using the subdivision of the beat, "1+2+3+4+". Then count and clap aloud to assist in assessing the off-beat feel of the rhythm.

Because the eighth note is a single eighth note and not paired with a second eighth note, a half beat begins the rhythmic figure. This causes the quarter note to be on the division of the beat, or the "+" (and), which subsequently emphasizes the division of the beat and displaces the downbeat stress, skewing the listener's sense of the downbeat. This example of syncopation can start on different beats of a measure depending on the meter in which it is found, and would occupy two beats total in a simple meter. Variations could also be possible, such as one of the notes being replaced with a rest instead, or the final eighth note being tied to a following note. This does not deter from the off-beat emphasis heard due to the rhythmic sequencing.

Suggested listening for eighth quarter eighth syncopation:

<u>Baroque</u> - Handel's "Water Music Suite IV. Hornpipe"

Syncopation can be found at the subdivision level also. A sixteenth-eighth-sixteenth syncopation sounds similar to the previous eighth-quarter-eighth syncopation, but at a shorter duration. If it were to occur on beat one, it would be counted as 1 <u>e+</u> a. Because the eighth note is sandwiched between sixteenths, the middle subdivisions underlined to indicate the joined durations. This rhythm can also be found on more beats than just the first in a measure, but the counting remains consistent. For example, 2 <u>e+</u> a is the same rhythmic sequence, just placed a beat later. This rhythmic figure would occupy one beat of space in a simple meter, and is treated similarly to the aforementioned syncopation at the division level, eight-quarter-eighth. A note in the sequence can be replaced with a rest, or tied to a note following the sequence, and it would still be considered syncopation because of how it displaces the typically anticipated emphasis of the stronger subdivisions.

Exercise 6.3

Rehearse exercise 6.3 with your metronome set to 50-60BPM. Before beginning, say the subdivisions aloud evenly distributing them within each click of the metronome. Then clap and count the syncopated rhythm.

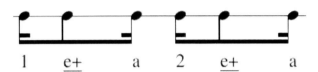

In compound meters, the use of syncopation is similar to simple meters. Any rhythmic sequence that emphasizes the weak beats is considered syncopation. Let's explore the application of syncopation in compound meters.

Recall that the beginning of every three-eighth-note grouping is the strong beat in compound meter. So, in 6/8 for example, beats one and four are the strong beats, and two, three, five, and six are the weak beats. If either or both of the strong beat notes were to be replaced with a rest, even-beat syncopation would occur. In 9/8, beats one, four, or seven could be replaced with a rest, and in 12/8, beats one, four, seven, or ten to create even-beat syncopation.

Exercise 6.4

In this exercise, each strong beat in 6/8 has been replaced with a rest. Rehearse this exercise using any metronome setting between 60-80 BPM. Whisper the counts on the rest to allot for their appropriate durations.

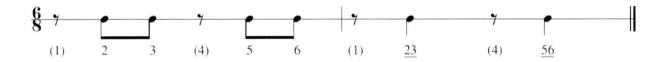

Like in simple meters, the strong beats can also be masked with ties over the bar line, or ties placed between the weak and strong beats can displace emphasis. For example, if beat three (weak beat) were to be tied to beat four (strong beat), beat four would be masked by the tie and not stressed as is typically expected. Or perhaps in 12/8, if beat twelve were tied over the bar line to the following downbeat, the downbeat would be masked. Quarter notes can also be placed strategically to create a syncopated feel that emulates the way ties mask the strong beats.

Exercises 6.5

Rehearse exercises 6.5 by clapping, tapping, count the durations of the ties carefully.

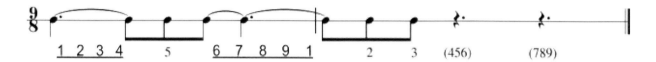

Syncopation is the most complex of the rhythm sequences studied thus far and will take time and practice to master. The more music you listen to that uses syncopation, the more fluent you will become at counting, feeling, and performing it accurately. Funk, Latin, Ragtime, and Jazz music feature an abundance of syncopated rhythms, and syncopation can be found in pop and rock as well.

Suggested listening for syncopation examples:

Funk – "Superstition" by Stevie Wonder
Latin – "La Vida Es Un Carnaval" by Celia Cruz
Ragtime – "The Maple Leaf Rag" by Scott Joplin

Day 7 – Tuplets

Rhythms discussed up to this point have been regular, rule-abiding sequences that fit into a predictable mold. In simple meters, the beat divides into two equal parts and can be subdivided into four equal parts. In compound meters, the beat divides into three equal parts and can be subdivided into six equal parts. Like most disciplines, there are outliers in rhythm that bring even more rhythmic possibilities; enter **tuplets.** Tuplets are any rhythm that is an abnormal division or subdivision of the beat that deviates from the expected division or subdivision determined by the time signature. They are irregular and "break the rules" so to speak. Tuplets can take multiple forms and are named after the division they create.

Duplet - two sounds
Triplet - three sounds
Quadruplet - four sounds
Quintuplet - five sounds
Sextuplet - six sounds
Septuplet - seven sounds
Octuplet - eight sounds
Nontuplet - nine sounds

In application, a tuplet occurs where a beat that would typically contain a certain division is made irregular. For example, the beat is typically divided into two equal parts in a simple meter. A specific tuplet called a **triplet** can be used, however, to defy the norm. A triplet is used to divide the beat into three equal parts rather than two. There can be half-note triplets, quarter-note triplets, eighth-note triplets, and sixteenth-note triplets.

Triplets are most commonly seen as an eighth-note triplet. An eighth-note triplet occupies one beat of duration. It is notated as three eighth notes grouped together with the number *3* below or above it to indicate its irregularity. An eighth-note triplet is best counted as 1-trip-let, or 2-trip-let, or 3-trip-let, etc. depending on the beat which it occurs.

Exercise 7.1

Set your metronome to a low BPM between 40-60. In Exercise 7.1, when you reach the measure with triplets, the goal is to divide each triplet figure evenly within one click. You may rehearse this measure separately to help achieve this.

Quarter-note triplets take two beats of duration to complete. This is irregular of course, and is notated with a bracket over the triplet quarter notes to group them since quarter notes cannot be beamed together and includes a number *3* above or below this bracket. The best way to count longer durations of triplets is to divide them into the next lower triplet division, which in this case would be eighth-note triplets. If we were to tie a pair of triplet-eighth notes together, they would be equivalent to a quarter-note triplet. In the example below, the measure on the left would be counted and played the same as the measure on the right.

Exercise 7.2

Use the counts from exercise 7.1 for the first measure of exercise 7.2. Go slowly and tie together the appropriate counts. When executed accurately, the first and second measure should sound the same because each individual triplet-quarter note receives two triplet-eighth notes.

Half-note triplets are created by dividing a whole note into three half notes. Whole notes regularly divide into two half notes, so it is irregular to have three half-note divisions. Because half notes cannot have a beam to group them together, a bracket with a three is used to notate that it is a triplet rather than usual half notes. A half-note triplet would be three sounds occupying four beats of duration. Again, use the next lower triplet division to decipher this rhythm. Quarter-note triplets tied into pairs are equivalent to the half-note triplet and best demonstrate how to feel the half-note-triplet figure.

When deciphering exercise 7.3 below, remember each part of the quarter-note triplet divides into two eighth-note triplets. Each part of the half-note triplet divides into two quarter-note triplets, so a single half-note triplet can be counted as four eighth-note triplets. The three half notes should be evenly split between four counts in the   measure.

Exercise 7.3

Tuplets can also be created from a division of the beat. An eighth note can be subdivided into three sixteenth notes to create a sixteenth-note triplet. This type of triplet would have three sixteenth notes beamed together with the number three above or below it to indicate it is a triplet figure. The total duration of a sixteenth note is a half of a beat in simple meter. They are likely to be found in a group of six in order to occupy a full beat. When grouped together as six over a beat, this rhythm can also be classified as a sextuplet. More on that momentarily.

While the triplet is the irregularity found in a simple meter, the **duplet** is the two-note division found in a compound meter. Remember, a compound meter regularly divides the beat into three even parts, and a duplet is the defiance of the norm for a compound meter. A duplet is most commonly used in compound meter as two eighth notes over one dotted-quarter-note beat, and is notated with the number two above or below the duplet to signify its abnormality. It would be counted as 1-and or 2-and or 3-and etc. depending on which dotted quarter note beat it occurs on within the measure.

Exercise 7.4

Set your metronome to 90-100 BPM and use the dotted quarter beat for exercise 7.4. This means there will be two clicks per measure. In the first measure, each click will fit three eighth notes, and in the second measure, each click will fit two eighth notes when executed properly. Feel free to rehearse the measure individually at first before transitioning between them. It may be helpful to imagine the second measure of rhythm as eighth notes in 2/4.

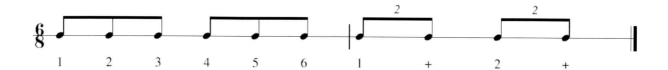

A **quadruplet** is a four-note grouping occupying the duration that three notes would regularly take of the same note type. A quadruplet-eighth-note figure would take the place of a grouping of three regular eighth notes. This would occur most commonly in compound meters. Because the beat is divided regularly into three eighth notes in compound meter, an eighth-note quadruplet could be used over the same duration. It would be counted as 1e+a (or 2e+a, or 3e+a etc.) depending on which dotted-quarter-note beat the quadruplet were to occur.

Exercise 7.5

Set your metronome to 90-100 BPM again and use the dotted-quarter beat for exercise 7.5. There will be three clicks per measure this time because of the triple 9/8 meter. In the first measure, each click will fit three eighth notes, and in the second measure, each click will fit four eighth notes when executed properly. Feel free to rehearse the measure individually at first before transitioning between them. It may be helpful to imagine the second measure as sixteenth notes in 3/4 time.

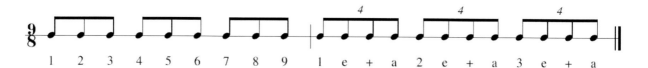

A quadruplet-half note is rare, but in theory would occupy the same space as three regular half notes. It could be used in 3/2 time to create a four-note feel within the bar. This crosses into **polyrhythm** territory, which for the purposes of this guide, will not be examined further. In depth study of music theory would offer more explanation to the properties of exceptional subjects like polyrhythm.

Quintuplets, sextuplets, and septuplets are treated the same with how they are divided into five, six, and seven notes within a given duration. In any tuplet beyond quadruplets, the tuplet will replace what would have regularly been four of the same note type. Regularly, there would be four sixteenth notes within a quarter-note duration, however a sixteenth-note quintuplet, sextuplet, septuplet, etc. could be used instead. Each would have the given number of notes beamed together with the appropriate number above or below to indicate the type of tuplet it is.

These tuplets can also be found as quarter notes and again would take the same space as four quarter notes, or four beats. Or as eighth notes occupying the same space as four eighth notes, or two beats.

Because there is an uneven number of sounds for quintuplets, the suggested way to count them is using five-syllable words and fitting the word within the allotted duration evenly. It is often easier to conceptualize the oddity of an uneven number beyond three with words. Hip-po-pot-a-mus is one of my favorites to use, but essentially, any five-syllable word will do the trick. You could also use 1-2-3-4-5 and evenly distribute the numbers within the duration of the quintuplet.

For any sextuplet, the standard counting procedure is 1-trip-let-and-trip-let to audibly discern the six sounds. Of course, feel free to use your own creativity and what works for you. Technically, any six-syllable word can be used to achieve the same results, as long as the syllables are evenly distributed within the allotted duration of the tuplet.

With any septuplet, I use the phrase "gold-en op-por-tu-ni-ty", but any seven-syllable word will work as long it flows evenly between the syllables. Some musicians use the phrase "lis-ten to these sev-en notes".

The higher the number within the tuplet is, the rarer it is. Beyond septuplet, the counting concepts remain consistent, and words and phrases will aid in counting them should you encounter them at any point. For the purpose of this guide, septuplets should be beyond what you will see for a long time, since these figures are seen in advanced, professional level music.

Overall, the most effective way to master counting and feeling any tuplet is to set the metronome to a very slow tempo, such as quarter note equals 50, or BPM=50. Practice tapping and saying the tuplet within one beat, then two, then three, then four depending on the note type the tuplet uses.

The following exercises feature quintuplets, sextuplets, and septuplets as quarter notes, eighth notes, and sixteenth notes in 4/4 time signature. Set your metronome to a slow BPM between 50-60 and try practice fitting each tuplet within the given duration. For example, for each initial measure, the tuplet should fit within four beats. For the second measure of each exercise, the tuplet should be distributed over two beats of the measure. And for the final measure of each, the tuplet should occur within one beat. Repeat as necessary to achieve mastery.

Exercise 7.6

Exercise 7.7

Exercise 7.8

If the last exercises proved difficult, don't worry. Quintuplets and septuplets are not all that common until you reach an advanced level of playing an instrument. On the contrary, triplets and sextuplets are more common.

Exercise 7.9

Rehearse today's final exercise, 7.9, for extra triplet practice. This time, the first measure quarter-note triplet must occur within two beats, the second measure eighth-note triplet must occur within one beat, and the third measure sixteenth-note triplets must occur within one beat as well. The sixteenth-note triplets in the final measure are equivalent to a sextuplet, being that there are six divisions in a single beat.

Congratulations on reaching the end of the first week of this guide! Upon completion of the first seven days, you should have a thorough understanding of pulse, notational structure, note values, counting, time signatures and meter. It is encouraged to frequently refer back to previous lessons as you progress into the second week. Regular practice and review of all concepts are essential to achieve complete understanding.

Week 1 Highlights

- Pulse is the steady heartbeat of music and can be set to faster and slower tempos.
- Music is structured into measures or bars, separated by bar lines, with equal amounts of beats within each measure. This is determined by the time signature found at the beginning of a musical piece or line.
- The time signature is notated with two stacked numbers. The top number indicates how many beats per measure, and the bottom number indicates what note type receives one beat.
- The relationship of strong and weak beats creates the rhythmic feel within a measure of music, and the downbeat is always the strongest beat of any given measure (unless it is masked with ties, replaced with a rest, or off-beat syncopation disrupts the flow).
- Note values determine the duration of sounds and silence. Note values discussed were whole notes, half notes, quarter notes, eighth notes, and sixteenth notes.
- Dots and ties provide additional note-value possibilities beyond the initial symbols by adding duration depending on the type of note to which the dot is attached.
- Counting of rhythmic sequences depends on if the music is in simple or compound meter, and what type of note receives the beat.
- Simple meters will always have a 2, 3, or 4 as the top number. Compound meters will always have a 6, 9, or 12 as the top number.
- Syncopation is a rhythmic sequence that displaces the anticipated emphasis of strong and weak beats and adds interest to the music.
- Tuplets defy the norm and create irregularity that also adds interest to music.

Week 2 – Pitch

Welcome to Week 2! This week's daily objectives will be centered around the musical element of pitch. The terms pitch and note are likely familiar terms to you, and they are often used synonymously. Before beginning our study of pitch, we first need to distinguish the difference between a pitch and a note.

Pitch refers to how high or low a sound is perceived. The highness or lowness of a pitch is measured using the frequency of its sound. In the physics of sound, frequency measures how many vibrations occur in a set amount of time. **Frequency** is measured with the number of wave cycles that occur within one second, and **Hertz** (abbreviated Hz) is the unit of measurement used to describe the frequency of a sound. The standard tuning system is set to A=440Hz. This is stipulating that the pitch "A" is measured at 440 Hz, and all pitches will be measured in relation to this.

While pitch is how high or low a sound is perceived by the ear, notes are the written forms of sound. Pitch is notated using notes, and notes are the visual representation of musical sounds in duration and frequency.

The instrument that offers the clearest visual representation of the relationship between pitches and notes is the piano keyboard. Although your chosen instrument may not be the piano, the piano keyboard is useful for seeing the way pitches work together to create music. There are several examples throughout this week that will use the keyboard as a visual aid when discussing universal music concepts.

There are numerous factors involved when notating pitch for specific instruments. This week will feature the most common and applicable symbols, terms, and strategies that are found in a majority of musical compositions. Additional study of your chosen instrument is encouraged and will coincide with this section of our guide.

Several exercises this week will require written answers. It is encouraged to write these answers down and then check the accuracy of your answer with the answer key at the end of the guide. Let's begin!

Day 8 - The Musical Alphabet

In order to organize pitch in music, the first seven letters of the alphabet, "A" through "G", are assigned at different frequency levels starting at 27.5 Hz, the lowest key on the piano (in practical ranges). There are significantly more than seven pitches possible in music of course, but because of how the science of sound works, these seven letters are grouped together into pitch classes that repeat within a pattern.

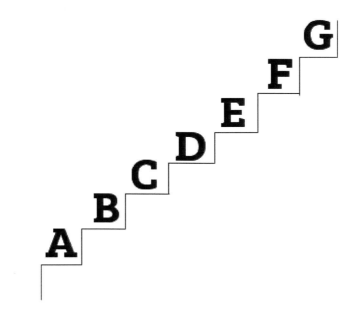

If the steps above continue past the top step, "G", the next step would be "A", and the sequence continues to repeat itself. Or, if while descending the alphabet steps below the first "A", the next step would be the letter "G" because we would be going backward in the sequence.

The white keys of the piano or keyboard best demonstrate how the musical alphabet sequences. Starting on the left, the lowest key on a full-size, 88-key piano is "A" at 27.5 Hz. As you can see, the musical alphabet continues in order, and after the seventh letter, "G", repeats itself until the end of the piano is reached at the far right, which is the highest pitch on piano. The highest pitch on a full 88-key keyboard or piano is a "C".

Although there are multiples of the same letter, these pitches do not sound the same. The lowest "A" on the piano is 27.5 Hz, while the next "A" in the sequence is at 55 HZ. Notes of the same letter classification are double the frequency of the previous, which creates a special relationship in sound. To distinguish the difference between pitches of the same letter name, or pitch class, they are assigned a **register** using a number. The lowest "A" is A0, and, from left to right, they continue A1, A2, A3, A4, A5, A6, and A7. A4 is at 440 Hz, which is the standard tuning system in modern music. The pitches following each "A" are given a number in the same fashion (ie. B0, C1, D1, C2, D2) with the number increasing as we move from left to right on the piano keyboard.

The black keys between and above the white keys are additional pitches, but they do not have any new letter names. Separate symbols are used to distinguish these pitches and will be discussed in depth on day ten of this week.

Exercises 8.1

Practice reciting the musical alphabet forward three times and backward three times without looking. Because music ascends and descends, it is important to be fluent in saying it backward as well as forward. Then, recite it forward and backward, starting and ending with the letters listed below. Use the stair-step image on the previous page as needed.

E to E   D to D   B to B   G to G   C to C   F to F

When relating the musical alphabet to your chosen instrument, its application varies depending on the instrument being played. The musical alphabet is universal in how you can use the letter names of notes to refer to specific pitches. For example, you may learn where to put your finger on the guitar to produce an "F" or what combination of fingers produces a "G" on the flute. For the purposes of this guide, we will focus on universal application of the musical alphabet and how to read its notation in the various forms you may encounter.

Exercise 8.2

Write down the answers to the following questions about today's reading. Check your answers on page 138.

1. How many letters are used to organize pitch in music?
2. Including register classification, what letter name would be the note after C1?
3. What letter comes after "G" in the musical alphabet?
4. What letter comes before "A" in the musical alphabet?
5. Are D2 and D3 considered to be of the same pitch class?

Day 9 - The Staff & Clefs

In the first week of this guide, notes were written on a single line to focus on timing and rhythm. Now that we are working with pitch as well, the full **staff** will be implemented. The musical staff is defined as five horizontal lines with four spaces between the lines.

The lines are numbered to help with identification, with line 1 as the bottom line, then line 2, line 3, line 4, and line 5 counting upward. The staff below has the lines numbered on the left side. The spaces between each line are also counted from the bottom, starting with space 1 above line 1, then space 2, space 3, and space 4. This is labeled on the right side of the staff below. When identifying a note, it is helpful to be able to distinguish which line or space the note is located.

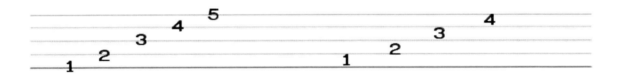

Pitches live on a staff as notes that can be written on these lines and spaces to notate their respective pitches. Notes on the staff are referred to as line notes or space notes according to their position on the staff. When written on a line, the note head will be directly on top of the line, and the line will appear to go through the center of the note head.

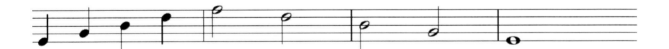

When notated on a space, the note head is written between the lines. Rather than being a line note, these are called space notes because they are written on the spaces between the lines.

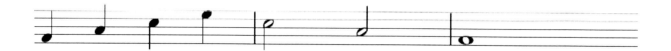

Exercise 9.1

On the staff below are several notes on various lines and spaces. On a sheet of paper, name which line or space the note head is written. Remember to start from the bottom and count up when determining which line or space. Answers can be checked with the answer key on page 138.

The location on the staff of a specific pitch depends on the clef or clefs that the music uses. Notes are spelled on the staff according to the clef. Clefs are found at the beginning of every piece of music, and there are several clefs that can be used. Let's begin with the **treble clef**.

Treble Clef

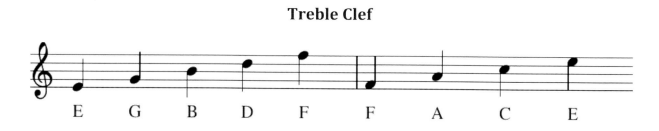

The treble clef is used for instruments with middle to higher ranges of pitch such as the flute, clarinet, saxophone, violin, guitar, soprano and alto voice types (sometimes tenor), and xylophone. It is also used for the notes on the right half of the keyboard, which is usually played with the right hand and higher in pitch. The lines and spaces on the treble clef staff are each assigned a letter name for the appropriate pitch to be notated. As shown above, the lines of the treble clef staff from bottom to top are E-G-B-D-F, and the spaces are F-A-C-E. Like the keyboard, from line to space starting on the bottom, the letters are alphabetical. The bottom line, "E", would be the home for the pitch E4. The top space, also "E", would be home for the pitch E5. The pitch of a note corresponds with how high or low it is written on the staff. Higher pitches will be written toward the top of the staff while lower pitches will be written toward the bottom of the staff respectively.

The treble clef is also called the G clef. When drawing a treble clef, there are specific places that the curves of the symbol are placed. Most importantly, the curl around the G-line is what refers to the treble clef being the G clef. Originally, the treble clef was called the G clef, because it circles the line determined to be "G" in this clef. Fun fact, the symbol itself is derived from an old way to write the letter "G". Some methods use this to identify notes by starting with the G-line 2 and using the alphabet to count up and down the staff. For example, using the musical alphabet, one could determine that the space above the G-line would be "A", and the space below the G-line would be "F", and continue in the sequence when identifying any given note.

When getting acclimated to note reading on the treble clef staff, many find it helpful to use a mnemonic for the line notes. A commonly used one is "Every Good Boy Does Fine", from bottom to top. I've also heard "Every Good Boy Deserves Fudge" or "Elephants Go Bouncing Down Freeways". Feel free to create your own mnemonic using the same letters to help you remember!

The spaces of the treble clef are easier to recall, since they spell the word FACE. Think FACE rhymes with SPACE to aid in memorizing. Be sure to always spell from bottom to top for accuracy. Notice again that when looking from line to space, the letters are alphabetical. Ascending up the staff is forward in the alphabet, and descending down the staff is reversed.

Exercise 9.2 - Treble Clef

Say the letter names of the lines five times fast while looking and then with your eyes closed. Do the same with the spaces.

On a sheet of paper, write the letter name for the following notes in the treble clef. Check your answers on page 139.

Bass Clef

G   B   D   F   A   A   C   E   G

The **bass clef** is used for instruments with low to middle ranges in pitch, such as the tuba, bass guitar, string bass, cello, euphonium, vocal bass, (sometimes vocal tenor), trombone and timpani drum. It is also used for notes on the left side of the keyboard, because they are lower in pitch. Like the treble staff, the lines and spaces all have designated letter names assigned for corresponding pitches to be notated. However, in the bass clef, the line and space letters are not in the same place as the treble clef. In bass clef, the bottom line, line one, is G2, and the top line, line 5, is A3. Essentially, the bass clef lines and spaces are the same as treble, but shifted down. As shown above, the lines from bottom to top are G-B-D-F-A, and the spaces are A-C-E-G.

The bass clef symbol is derived from an old way to write the letter "F", so it is also named the F clef. The two dots surrounding line four of the bass clef staff is the F-line in this clef (F3 specifically). This information offers an additional method that can be used to identify notes by going forward and backward in the musical alphabet when moving up and down from line to space on the F clef/bass clef staff.

The commonly shared mnemonic for the lines of the bass clef is "Good Boys Do Fine Always" or "Good Boys Deserve Fudge Always." A personal favorite is "Grizzly Bears Don't Fly Airplanes." As always, feel free to create a mnemonic of your own using the same letters in the same order.

The spaces of the bass clef are not quite as convenient as the in treble clef is with FACE, so a mnemonic is once again useful to assist in identification. "All Cows Eat Grass" and "All Cars Eat Gas" are a couple to choose from, or create your own if you'd like!

Exercise 9.3 - Bass Clef

Say the letter names of the lines from bottom to top five times fast while looking and then with your eyes closed. Do the same with the spaces.

Now, write the letter names for the following notes in the bass clef. Check your answers on page 139 of the answer guide.

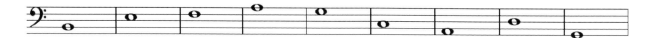

Because the piano has an expansive range of pitches and uses two hands, piano music uses two separate staves. Piano music uses both the treble clef and bass clef combined into the **grand staff**.

Grand Staff

Notice the brace joining the two staves together on the far left. Music written on either or both staves will occur simultaneously from left to right. Pianists typically have ten fingers and two hands, and so the instrument allows for two simultaneous musical lines. Harp, organ, and marimba also use the grand staff.

You may be wondering how all of the pitches analyzed on the piano keyboard yesterday would fit within the treble and bass clef staves. From the bottom line to the top line of each, there would only be enough spots for nine notes total, eighteen when combined. Because there are many more pitches possible, music is written beyond the staff as well. First, the spaces above and below the top and bottom lines of the staff are used to notate additional space notes. Notes on these spaces would be the next pitch in

the alphabet if above staff or the previous pitch in the alphabet if below the staff.

Beyond that, shorter lines are added to continue the space-line pattern. These shorter lines that create additional lines beyond the staff are called **ledger lines**.

Ledger lines operate in the same way the rest of the staff does. When multiple lines are used, they are spaced equally. The space between the ledger lines can also be used for additional space notes. As we move from line to space going up beyond the top line, the notes will continue forward in the musical alphabet. As notes move down below the bottom line, the lines and spaces are lettered going backward in the music alphabet.

Exercise 9.4

The following ledger line notes are in the treble clef. On a separate sheet of paper, write the letter name of each. Remember the top line of the treble clef staff is "F", and the bottom line is "E". Check your answers on page 139.

Exercise 9.5

The following ledger line notes are in the bass clef. On a separate sheet of paper, write the letter name of each. Remember the top line of the bass clef staff is "A", and the bottom line is "G". Check your answers on page 139.

The treble and bass clef are the most commonly used clefs in music. There is an additional group of clefs used in some instances called the C clefs. The **C clef** is a movable clef. The symbol can be placed in different positions on the staff to create five individual clefs. The curved portion of the symbol that comes to a point signifies the location of Middle C, or C4, on the staff. This point is moved up and down the staff to establish which line Middle C will be notated. The five locations of the C clefs were primarily used in vocal music prior to the 20th century. Simply put, their purpose was to avoid using ledger lines. In modern music, two of the five are seen in orchestral music. We will discuss these two starting with the **alto clef.**

 Nowadays, the alto clef is used for the viola of the orchestral instruments, a specialty instrument called the alto trombone, and the mandola.

Alto Clef

| F | A | C | E | G | G | B | D | F |

The symbol is classified as a C Clef because the line on which it is centered establishes the location of Middle C. In alto clef, this is line three in the center of the staff. From there, the sequence of the musical alphabet remains the same as treble or bass clef. It is just shifted to a new location on the staff for alto clef.

Exercise 9.6

Identify the letter name for the following notes on the alto clef staff below. Write your answers on a sheet of paper and check for accuracy with the answer key on page 139 of the answer key.

The **tenor clef** is occasionally used for the upper register of instruments that also use the bass clef, such as the trombone, bassoon, and cello.

Tenor Clef

| D | F | A | C | E | E | G | B | D |

Tenor clef also uses the C clef symbol; however, the clef is centered on line 4 of the staff, establishing this as the Middle C line. Notes can then be determined using the musical alphabet starting with either going forward from "C" if counting up, or backward from "C" if counting down.

Exercise 9.7

Identify the letter name for each note on the tenor clef staff below. Write your answers on a sheet of paper. Check your answers with the answer key on page 139.

When notes are written on any staff, the stem direction is determined by how far up or down the note is notated. The middle line of any staff, line 3, is the turning point for the stems. When a stemmed note is on or above line 3, the stem goes down. When a stemmed note is on or below line 3 of the staff, the stem goes up. See the image below for clarification.

The treble clef (G clef), bass clef (F clef), alto clef (C clef), and tenor clef (C clef) are all clefs that notate pitch as notes on the musical staff. There are a few specialty clefs to mention that are used for percussion and popular string instruments as well.

Percussion clef is used for unpitched percussion instruments like snare drum, bass drum, cymbals, auxiliary percussion, and drum set. Pitch is not notated for these instruments because they do not have pitch classifications to play. The sounds these instruments make are considered unpitched. The lines and spaces of the staff are used uniquely in percussion clef to indicate which instrument is sounding.

The example below is in percussion clef; i.e., the two short, bold, vertical lines at the far left are the percussion clef. This music is drum-set music. The lines and spaces of the staff are assigned instruments to play as a part of the drum set, such as kick drum on the bottom space, tom-toms on the center notes, and cymbal crashes on the "x" note heads.

Guitar, Bass Guitar, and Ukulele **tablature**, or **tab** for short, are also instrument specific notations with their own style of "staff". Guitar tablature uses six lines for the six strings and notates pitch using fret numbers of the guitar. Bass guitar and ukulele do the same, but with four lines for their four strings.

Day 10 - Half Steps & Accidentals

Today we are going to deepen our understanding of how notes move and relate to each other. When notes move from a line to the very next space up or down, or from a space to the very next line up or down, this is called a step. A step will change the note by one letter name, such as "A" to "B", or "G" to "F". "C" steps up to "D", and "A" steps down to "G". It is useful when learning to read music and play an instrument or sing to be able to identify steps and their direction.

A step can be further classified into two categories: **half step** and **whole step**. A half step is the distance between any two pitches consecutively next to each other. This is best visualized with the piano keyboard again. The image below is a part of the piano keyboard. The blue arrows are pointing to keys that are a half step apart.

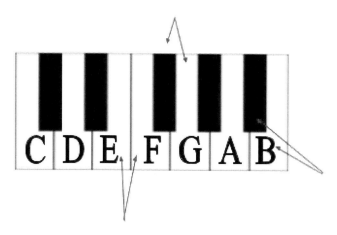

Remember when we were studying the musical alphabet in Day 9, and we exclusively examined the white keys and omitted the black keys? Those pitches are going to become a part of our half step discussion today. Using the keyboard image above, notice how black keys are found between most of the white keys. Let's examine the white keys "A" and "B", and the black key between. The pitch of that black key would be a half step between the pitches "A" and "B". Now find "E" and "F". There is no black key, so "E" and "F" are considered to be half step apart. "B" and "C" are the same as "E" and "F" in regard to being a half step apart.

Notes can move up or down by half steps, and there are symbols used to indicate their direction. The **sharp sign** indicates that the note is to be played a half step higher. On the keyboard, this would be the key directly to the right of the given pitch. For example, if the lettered note were to be an "A sharp", the black key directly to the right of "A" would be played because it is a half step higher. The symbol for a sharp sign is the same as the pound sign or hashtag, and is found directly before the note it belongs to on the staff.

Notice that it is centered on the same line or space that the note to which it is attached. If the measure above were in treble clef, the note would be named a "C" sharp (C#), raising the pitch "C" by a half step. The sound of the pitch would be slightly higher than "C" and can be thought of as the halfway point between "C" and "D".

As mentioned previously, there are places where there is not a black key between white keys on the keyboard. This is because E-F and B-C are naturally occurring half steps. If an "E sharp" (E#) were written in music, it would be played as "F" because "F" is a half step higher than "E". "B#" would be played as "C" for the same reason.

Exercises 10.1

On a sheet of paper, draw a staff (five horizontal lines across the page). Draw a sharp sign on each line and each space of the staff.

While sharp signs indicate to play the note a half step higher, the **flat sign** indicates that the note is to be played a half step lower. On the keyboard, this is the key directly to the left of the given pitch. A flat sign symbol is similar to a lowercase "b".

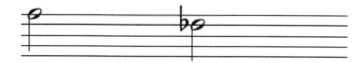

Notice that like the sharp sign, the flat sign is centered on the same line or space as the note to which it belongs, and it is written prior to the note as well. The pitch of the flatted note will sound slightly lower. If the measure above were in treble clef, the second note would be a "D flat" (Db).

In the places previously mentioned without a black key, the flat sign would function the same. "F flat" (Fb) is "E" because "E" is a half step below "F". "C" flat would be "B" for the same reason.

Exercise 10.2

On a sheet of paper, draw a staff. On each line and space of the staff, draw a flat sign.

You may have noticed that there are now two names for the many notes of the same pitch, a flat name and a sharp name. These notes are called **enharmonic** equivalents. This means that there is more than one name for the same pitch. For example, "A#" is the enharmonic equivalent to "Bb" because it is a half step higher than "A" and a half step lower than "B". There are multiple names for the same pitch.

Exercise 10.3

On a sheet of paper, copy the keyboard image below. Label all of the white keys using letter names. Then, label the black keys using both the flat and sharp letter names for each. The first white key and first black key are labeled to get you started. Check your accuracy with the answer key on page 140.

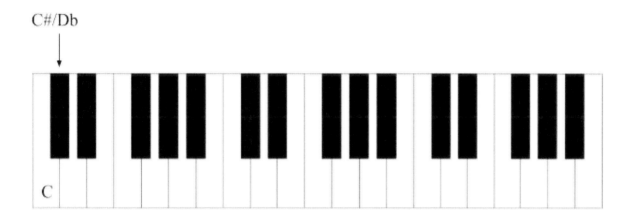

When written on the staff in music, the sharp and flat signs have a rule. They always carry through the measure to any other notes on the same line or space as the initial marked sharp or flat. The measure following the measure with the flat or sharp sign, however, would reset and the notes in that measure would not be affected.

Exercise 10.4

Determine how many flat notes are in the first measure, and how many sharp notes are in the second measure. Write your answers on a sheet of paper and check the answer key on page 140.

What if a composer didn't want the sharp or flat to carry through the measure? What if they wanted a regular "B" after the "B flat"? Or a regular "C" after the "C sharp"? There is a symbol that notates to cancel a flat or sharp called a **natural sign**.

A natural sign cancels any sharp or flat and indicates to play the natural given pitch, such as "B" or "C" rather than "Bb" or "C#". In the first measure of the image above, the natural sign cancels the previous sharp sign. In the second measure, the natural sign cancels the previous flat sign. Had the natural signs not been included, the sharp and flat would have carried through to the next note. Natural signs also carry through the measure to any note of the same pitch class, like sharps and flats.

Exercise 10.5

Determine how many sharp vs. natural notes are in the first measure, and how many flat vs. natural notes are in the second measure. Every note will be counted. Check your answers with the key on page 140.

Flats, sharps, and naturals are collectively called **accidentals.** They are all alterations to the pitch they are attached to in some manner. To review, sharps raise the pitch a half of a step, flats lower a pitch a half of a step, and naturals cancel out a flat or a sharp.

When notes move by two half steps, this is called a whole step. To put it simply, two halves make a whole. "A" to "B" is an example of a whole step because, starting at "A", we would move up two half steps to get to "B". The arrows in the next keyboard image point between keys that are a whole step apart.

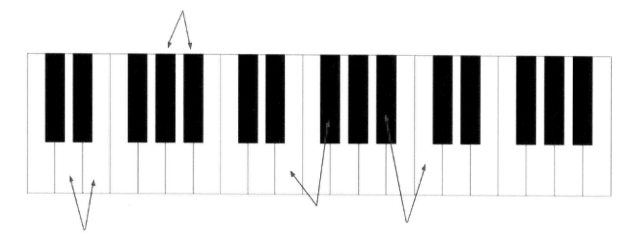

Half and whole steps will continue to be explored when we study intervals tomorrow. It is useful to identify when notes are changing by steps on the staff to aid in fluency in reading in any given clef with any instrument.

Exercise 10.6

Practice identifying the distance between the following letter names as half or whole steps. Assume that the notes are next to each other on the staff. Use the keyboard images above to assist. Also include if the direction of the step is up or down when writing your answer. For example, for "A" to "B", the answer would be "whole step up". Feel free to write your answers on a sheet of paper and check yourself with the answer key on page 140.

on page 140.

A to B   *Db to C*   *A to G#*   *Bb to C*   *E to F*   *D# to E*

Day 11 – Intervals

In musical terms, an **interval** is the distance between two consecutive or simultaneous notes. Becoming skilled in recognizing the distance between notes on the musical staff by sight will contribute to your musical literacy. It aids in transitioning between notes fluently, which will ensure you stay in time while playing or singing.

When measuring the distance between pitches or notes, the amount of distance between each note is classified as an interval. Intervals are represented using numerical values that measure their distance. For example, notes between two of the same pitch classes can be a second (2nd), third (3rd), fourth (4th), fifth (5th), sixth (6th), seventh (7th), or eighth (8th) apart. Notes that are closer together will have a smaller interval number, and notes that are further apart will have a larger interval number. The distance can continue beyond an 8th, but for today, we are going to study intervals within an 8th.

Let's begin with the interval of a 2nd. When two notes are directly next to each other on the staff, they are a 2nd apart. The whole and half steps examined yesterday are both examples of 2nds. To determine the distance between any two notes, the initial notes is counted as "one" and the following note "two". So "C" to "D" would be a 2nd because "C" is step one, then "D" is step two. On the staff below are two ways 2nds can be found. On the left is the melodious interval, and on the right is the harmonic interval. An interval is melodious when each pitch is sounded separately, or one at a time. Harmonic refers to when the notes occur simultaneously, as pictured on the right. Notice that because of the close proximity of the notes, they are notated on opposite sides of the stem to give space for each note head.

Interval - Seconds - 2nds

Some instruments can only play one note at a time, while instruments like the piano or guitar can sound multiple pitches simultaneously, so we will use examples of melodic and harmonic versions of each interval. The interval of a 2nd is essentially a step, but it is useful to also identify them this way as we expand into intervals beyond steps.

The next interval after the 2nd would be the 3rd. A 3rd is like two steps on the staff and is often referred to as a skip, because it will skip one letter or one note on the staff. The distance between the note "C" and the note "E" would be a 3rd, and to play this interval we would skip over the note "D".

Interval - Thirds - 3rds

Notice how the notes on the staff above are a line-to-line apart, or a space-to space apart. This is a quick way to identify that the notes are a 3rd apart. In the harmonic interval example on the right side, the notes are stacked neatly because the distance between the notes allows room for the note heads.

Exercise 11.1

For each measure below, determine if the notes are a 2nd or 3rd apart. On a sheet of paper, write the interval names (e.g. 2nd, 3rd, etc.). Check your answers on page 140 of the answer key.

2nds and 3rds are easy to identify by sight because they are, simply put, steps and skips, and closer together on the staff. The next interval beyond a 3rd is a 4th. A 4th will appear as a line to space on the staff or a space to a line, but not directly next to each other. Remember to count the initial note as step one.

<h3 style="text-align:center">Interval - Fourths - 4ths</h3>

Fifths will be written from line to line or space to space with an empty line or space between, respectively. You can also think of a 5th like a double skip, moving from line to line to line, or space to space to space.

<h3 style="text-align:center">Interval - Fifths - 5ths</h3>

Exercise 11.2

For each measure below, determine if the notes are a 4th or 5th apart. On a sheet of paper, write the interval names (e.g. 4th, 5th, etc.). Check your answers on page 140.

Notes that are a 6th apart will be written from line to space or space to line, one step further than a 5th. You can also think of the interval of a 6th like a double skip, plus one.

<h3 style="text-align:center">Interval - Sixths - 6ths</h3>

The interval of a 7th is seen as notes that are both found on lines or both found on spaces like the 3rd or 5th, but even further. If the notes are on lines, there will be two skipped lines between the notes, or if on spaces there will be two empty spaces between the notes. A 7th can be thought of like a triple skip.

Exercise 11.3

For each measure below, the notes are either a 3rd, 5th, or 7th apart. On a sheet of paper, write the interval of the notes in each measure. Check your answers on page 141.

The word **octave** is derived from a Latin root meaning "eight" and is used in music as another name for the interval of an 8th. Notes that are an octave apart are of the same pitch class, meaning they are the same letter name. The distance between the pitch C4 and the pitch C5 would be considered an octave. The word octave is used more often than the word 8th, and they are equivalent. On the staff, an octave will appear as a one note on a line and the other on a space, or vice versa. It will be a seventh plus one step.

Interval - Eighth - 8ths - Octave

Because the octave is frequently used in music, there are markings that indicate to play a note or passage of notes up or down an octave. The most commonly used, *8va* is the abbreviation for the Italian phrase "**all' ottava**", or "at the octave". This marking is usually found above specified notes on the staff to be played an octave higher than written, and is sometimes accompanied with a dashed line to indicate how long the passage is to be played up the octave. When printed below the staff, this marking indicates for the notes to be played an octave lower than written. *8vb,* meaning "at the octave below" is a similar marking is also used to indicate the octave below.

In the top line in the image above, the *8va* sign is above the staff with a dotted line bracket indicating to play those specified notes up an octave from written. To the right of the double bar line are the notes that would be sounded. The second line of music presents the 8va sign beneath the staff with the dotted line bracket. This indicates for the specified notes to be played down an octave. An 8vb could also be used in this situation, "**ottava bassa**". The notes to the right of the double bar line are what would be sounded when played.

The markings *15ma* and *15mb* are used in the same way as the octave markings. 15ma means to play the indicated notes two octaves higher, and 15mb means to play the indicated notes two octaves lower. You may wonder why it isn't 16 rather than 15. This is because the interval of two octaves is a 15th, not a sixteenth.

C	D	E	F	G	A	B	C	D	E	F	G	A	B	C
1	2	3	4	5	6	7	8	9	10	11	12	13	14	15

There is also a term for when two consecutive notes are of the same pitch. This is called a perfect **unison**. Notes in unison will be the same exact pitch and the same letter name.

Exercise 11.4

The notes in each measure below can be of any interval discussed today. On a sheet of paper, write the interval of the notes in each measure. Check your answers on page 141.

Day 12 – Scales

A **scale**, in music, is defined as any graduated sequence of notes, tones, or intervals dividing an octave. Recall from yesterday we learned that an octave is the interval of an 8th, which is the distance between two notes of the same pitch class and letter name (e.g. C to C). Scales are written with a sequence of half and whole steps in order to give them a particular sound. We learned in Day 10 that a half step is the distance between any two consecutive pitches. A whole step is simply two half steps.

There are numerous pitch/note combinations possible within an octave when including all of the half step and whole step sequences available. Different cultures and parts of the world use certain scales that give their music a distinguishable sound. Without delving too deeply into music theory, we are going to analyze the most commonly used scales in modern music today.

Let's begin our scale discussion with the analysis of the two most commonly used scale modes, major and minor. Most commonly, a scale will have seven different pitch classes moving up and down in steps, and in total contain eight notes, with the first and last being of the same pitch class. For example "C-D-E-F-G-A-B-C" is seven different pitch classes, with the first and last being of the same pitch class an octave apart. A scale can be built starting on any pitch class.

Major scales and **minor scales** are both stepwise arrangements of seven pitches forming an octave. These pitches are classified into **scale degrees**, which are numbers used to designate each step of the scale. For example, in a "C" major or minor scale, "C" is the first scale degree, D is the second scale degree, etc.

Each scale has a certain sound that music uses to invoke a particular mood and pattern. This is created by how the notes are sequenced regarding whether each step increases by a half or a whole step. Each scale is composed of a sequence of half and whole steps that create its sound. To be major, the formula for the sequence is "whole-whole-half-whole-whole-whole-half."

Major Scale Formula

W-W-H-W-W-W-H

Let's apply this formula starting on the pitch "C". In the image below, the whole and half steps are labeled in the boxes pointing between the corresponding keys on the piano.

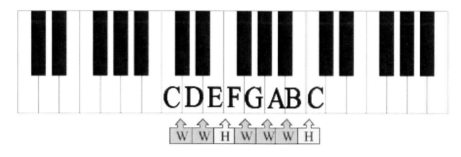

The C Major scale has no sharps or flats because the notes naturally lay out to fit the formula. It is the only major scale that won't have a single sharp or flat in it.

If we use the major scale formula starting on any pitch class, the major scale of that pitch class will be created. Let's build a scale starting on the pitch "F".

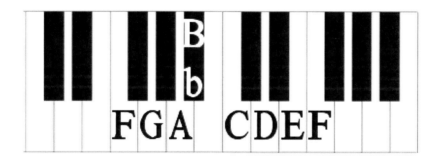

In order for the sequence of notes to adhere to the major scale formula, this scale requires a B flat. With that alteration, the whole steps and half steps are all in the proper place for a major scale.

Exercise 12.1

Build an ascending major scale starting on the pitch "G", using the major scale formula to determine the sequence of letter names. There will be one sharp note needed in this scale to fit the major scale formula. Check your answer with page 141.

It is beneficial to get acquainted with the sounds of major and minor music. The following listening suggestion is a famous French folk song. This same tune will be altered in the minor listening example coming up in this section.

Suggested listening for major scale sounds:

<u>French Folk Song</u> – "Frère Jacques"

Minor scales are built similarly to major scales, but the half steps occur in a different part of the formula, changing the sound of the scale. The formula for the minor scale is "Whole-Half-Whole-Whole-Half-Whole-Whole."

Let's apply this formula starting on the pitch "A".

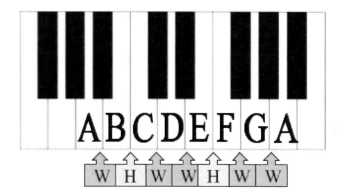

An "A" Minor scale has no flats or sharps just like C Major. "A" Minor is the only minor scale without a sharp or flat needed to create it. C Major and A Minor are relative to each other because of this commonality. Every major scale has a relative minor that contains the same flatted or sharped note(s).

Let's now build a minor scale that requires an accidental. The E Minor scale is pictured on the piano keyboard directly below. In order for the notes to fit the minor scale half step and whole step sequence, one sharp, F#, is required.

Exercise 12.2

Build an ascending minor scale starting on the pitch "D" using the minor scale formula to determine the sequence of letters. You will need to flat one of the pitches in order for it to fit the formula. Check your answer on page 141.

The following suggested listening uses the tune from Frere Jacques as a funeral march. The composer altered the whole and half step sequence of the original tune to give the music the minor sound.

Suggested listening for minor scale sounds:

Classical – "Symphony No. 1 Mov. 3" by Gustav Mahler

Every major or minor scale has a specific number of flats or sharps. The examples examined above contained either no flats or sharps or a single flat or sharp. Each major and minor scale equivalent built on their respective pitch class will have their own unique number of accidentals (flats or sharps). A scale will not mix flats and sharps, so it will either have sharps or flats, not both.

The minor scale can take different forms that are created by adding accidentals from outside of the scale formula. The natural form of the minor scale is what is produced when using the formula. It is appropriately called the **natural minor scale.** It is the simplest form of the minor scale because it fits the formula without alterations.

When the 7th degree of the scale is raised by a half step, the most popular form of the minor scale is created, the **harmonic minor scale.** Because of the half step between the last two notes of the scale with the added raised pitch, anticipation is created, and the resolutions of the scale and musical patterns are perceived as more cohesive. Most minor music uses the harmonic minor scale.

Two additional types of scales to mention today are the chromatic scale and pentatonic scales. A **chromatic scale** is a twelve-note sequence consisting of half steps only. It can start on any given pitch class and will extend an octave. It will essentially include every pitch possible within the octave in order of ascension. The following image spans two octaves of the C chromatic scale, starting and ending with "C".

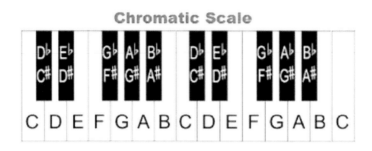

Suggested listening for chromatic scale sounds:

Classical – "Flight of the Bumblebee" by Nikolai Rimsky-Korakov

Conversely, the **pentatonic scale** is a five-note sequence that excludes any half steps. This creates a uniquely pure sound that is predominantly found in Eastern and in European folk music. An example of a pentatonic scale would be "C-D-E-G-A-C". The omittance of "F" and "B" within the octave removes any half steps.

Suggested listening for pentatonic scale sounds:

Chinese traditional – "The Fisherman's Song at Dusk" by Hong Ting

Scales are the foundation on which music is written, and their practice will aid you in reading and hearing music more fluently. Nearly every piece of music you may encounter uses the notes of a particular scale to create the musical sounds. Practice of scales on your instrument will train your fingers, hands, eyes, and/or voice in preparation for these note sequences and combinations.

Day 13 - Key Signatures

You may recall from Week 1 that we studied how music is structured regarding bar lines and meter. At the beginning of any piece of music, there is a clef, a time signature, and in between each of those is the **key signature**. The key signature notates the key of the entire song or section of a song. Before discussing the key signature, let's first elaborate on the **key** of the music.

Yesterday we took a glance at scales. Every scale started and ended on the same pitch class and contained notes in a particular sequence within the octave. The first note of each scale is considered the "home note" of the scale. When a song or musical piece is written, the notes of a given scale typically predetermine the structure of the tune. Basically, the composer selects notes of the scale to create the music. Each note serves a function in the composition, but for the purposes of this guide, the most important to distinguish is the "home note", or the starting pitch class of each scale. For example, in a C Major scale, "C" is the "home note". When a musical piece is written based around the C Major scale, it is in the key of "C".

The key of a musical composition is notated with the key signature using the flats or sharps that would be found in that scale. Both the C Major scale and the A Minor scale have no flats or sharps, so a composition in one of these keys would have a blank key signature. This notifies the musician that the given piece of music is either in C Major or its relative minor, A Minor. The key signature of a minor scale is its natural form. The key signature is notated between the clef and the time signature. In the examples below, only the clef and time signature are used because these are all examples of the blank key signature, C major or A minor.

To distinguish if a blank key signature is major or minor depends on whether the notes in the music are written using A Minor scale patterns or C Major scale patterns. Analyzing, performing, and listening to the pattern of notes in a piece of music will likely clarify if the music is major or minor. Many describe music in a major key to be joyful, uplifting, fun, or angelic. Minor key music is often described as somber, sinister, spooky, or occasionally adventurous.

The visual way to determine if music is major or minor is to analyze the notes in the music. The "home note" of the key will be seen, played, or heard frequently and oftentimes be the final note of a composition. This is because that initial pitch of a scale has a settling sound, or a finality to it, that is nearly always adhered to when music is written. In-depth study of music theory and music composition offer further explanation and analysis of the relationship between notes and determining the key of a song. To begin, it is best to memorize every key signature and practice the major and minor scale affiliated with each.

Key signatures can also contain flats or sharp, but never both simultaneously. Like scales, if the key has any alterations, they will either be all sharps or all flats. There is also a sequence for the placement of each sharp or flat. The key signature of one sharp is pictured below in treble, bass, alto, and tenor clef.

These are the key signatures of G Major and the relative E Minor. In each clef, the sharp sign is located on the F-line of the staff. This sharp indicates that all F's are sharp. This key signature belongs exclusively to those keys (within major and minor music) and is the only key with one sharp. That sharp will always be F sharp because that is the sharp needed for the G Major and E Minor scales. As key signatures gain sharps, the sharps always appear in the following order: F sharp, C sharp, G sharp, D sharp, A sharp, and B sharp.

Sharp Key Signatures

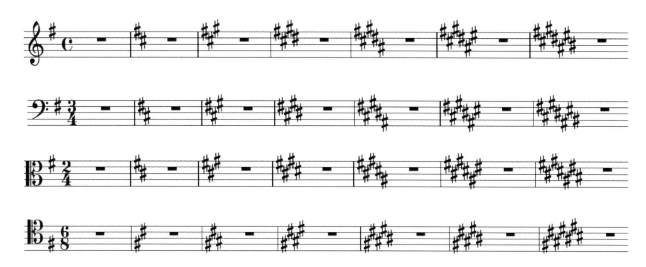

If a key signature contains a flat or flats, the flat(s) apply to all pitches of the letter name of the lines and/or spaces the flat is found. The key signature of one flat is pictured below.

This is the key signature of F Major and the D Minor. Both of the F Major and D Minor scales contain a B flat. The key signature of one flat, B flat, will exclusively be either F Major or D Minor (among major and minor music). That single flat will always be B flat. As flats are added to the key signature, the order of the flats will be B flat, E flat, A flat, D flat, G flat, C flat, and F flat.

Flat Key Signatures

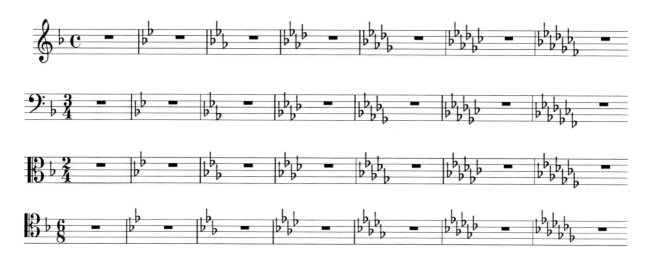

With any given key signature except the blank key, the flat(s) or sharp(s) marked applies to all notes of that pitch class found in the music following the key signature. So, in the key of G Major, all F's are sharp, in any octave, even if they're not on the same line the sharp is written in the key signature. The musician would only play F natural if a natural sign were notated on an F in the music. This natural sign would cancel out the key signature for that note and any other F's until the next measure.

There are twelve pitch classes total when counting every pitch within an octave, and subsequently there are twelve major and twelve minor key signatures, one of each for each pitch class. A diagram used to understand and memorize all of these is using the "Circle of Fifths" and the "Circle of Fourths".

The Circle of Fifths

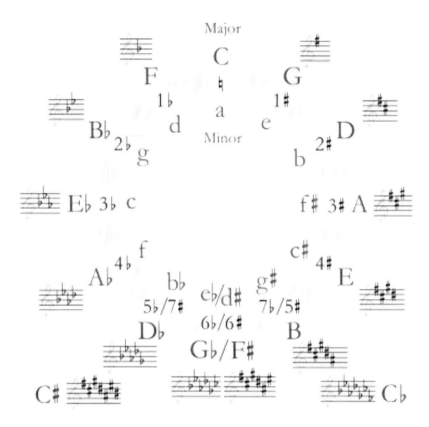

This circle uses the treble clef to notate each key signature. On the right side of the **Circle of Fifths** are sharps, and on the left side are flats. On the outer part of the circle are the major key letter names, and on the inner part of the circle are the minor key letter names. At the top of the circle, we see the key signature for C Major/A Minor. As you look to the right around the circle, or clockwise, the next key signature is G Major/E Minor. When listing pitches in letter name order, C to G and A to E would both be a fifth apart. The Circle of Fifths lists the keys using the interval of a fifth to progress to the next key signature, starting with C major/A minor.

At the bottom of the circle are the key signatures of G flat and F sharp Major together, and their relative minor keys, E flat Minor and D sharp Minor. Remember enharmonic notes from Day 10? G flat and F sharp are two letter names for the same pitch. E flat and D sharp are also enharmonic equivalents. So, these key signatures are two different ways to write the same major scale and two different ways to write the same minor scale.

Exercise 13.1

Using the formula for a major scale, WWHWWWH, on a sheet of paper write out the Gb (flat) Major scale in letters, and the F# (sharp) Major scale in letters. Check your scale accuracy with the answer key on page 141.

The Circle of Fourths

The sides of the circle are swapped in the **Circle of Fourths.** The key signatures containing flats are on the right side, and the keys with sharps are on the left side of the circle. The outer, capital letters are the major key names and the inner, lowercase letters are the minor equivalents. The blank key signature, C Major/A Minor, is again at the top of the circle. Progressing to the right of the circle, each key adds a flat until, once again at the bottom, there's the transition to sharps. The next key letter name, going to the right, or clockwise, is the interval of a fourth up from the previous. "C" to "F" is a fourth, "F" to "Bb" is a fourth, and this pattern continues around the Circle of Fourths.

Some may find keeping track of the Circle of Fourths or Fifths overwhelming, and if so, fear not. There are a few shortcuts that may expedite the process of memorizing and recognizing key signatures.

For sharps, the last sharp in the key signature is a half step below the major key affiliated with that key signature. For example, if the key signature has two sharps, the final sharp listed from left to right is "C#". "C#" is a half step below "D", and the major key with two sharps is D Major. This method will work to determine any major key signature.

Exercise 13.2

Name the note that would be a half step above the given sharp pitches named below. Write your responses on a sheet of paper and consult with the answer key on page 141 upon completion.

F#   C#   G#   D#   A#   E#

For flats, the second to last flat listed in the key signature is the name of the major key affiliated with the key signature. For example, in a key signature with three flats, the flats are listed as "Bb", "Eb", and "Ab", in that particular order. The second to last flat is "Eb", and that is the major key for this key signature.

Exercise 13.3

The number of flats mentioned in each example below are part of a key signature. Determine what the second to last flat would be in each example. Remember the flats are always listed in this order: Bb, Eb, Ab, Db, Gb, Cb, Fb. Write your responses on a separate sheet of paper, and check your answers on page 141.

2 flats - 3 flats - 4 flats - 5 flats - 6 flats - 7 flats

Using that method for identifying a flat signature works for all the flat key signatures except the key with one flat. Because it is a single flat, there is not a second to last flat. That key will have to be memorized as F Major/D Minor.

Those two methods will only reveal the major key that the piece of music might be in, but there is also the possibility of the music being in the relative minor key. The simplest way to determine what minor scale matches the key is to first determine the major key name using one of the two most recently discussed methods using the last sharp or second to last flat accordingly. Second, determine the sixth note of that major scale. In a C Major scale, the sixth note would be an "A". The relevant minor key is therefore, A Minor.

Exercise 13.4

For each major key listed below, write the relative minor key. Check your answers with the answer key on page 141 of the answer key.

D Major   Ab Major   F Major   C Major   Db Major   B Major

If all else fails, look at the Circle of Fourths or the Circle of Fifths as a reference for any key you encounter. A key signature will always be included in any music you play, even if it is blank. In fact, music can even change the key at any point. When a key change occurs in sheet music, the clef with key signature alterations will appear at the place in time of the new key.

As a musician, it is, at minimum, essential that you understand how to apply a key signature. You must be able to identify which line or space the sharps or flats in the key signature are notated, understand that this applies to all notes of the same pitch class, and perform the music accordingly. Missing the key signature will cause the music to sound off because the notes will be incorrect unless the key signature is observed properly. That is where the expression "off-key" stems from.

Many beginners find it helpful to write the letter names of the flats or sharps above the key signature. It is also common practice to mark a note with a flat or sharp in the music as needed for occasional reminders of the key signature.

Day 14 - Melody, Harmony, & Chords

When music is composed, there are often several layers within the music regarding principal and secondary parts or lines. The role of a given musical line depends on the arrangement of the music. As a player or singer, distinguishing what role your part serves at any given moment will produce a more polished performance.

We often hear the word **melody** associated with music, but what exactly is a melody? The melody of a composition is a musically satisfying sequence of notes that serve as the principal part. It is often described as the "tune", and in a song is the line that is sung, or the line we might hum or whistle. Melodies frequently have themes that reoccur in a musical piece. The easiest way to distinguish a melody in music is by listening. The music is centered around the melody and our ears will be drawn to it.

Suggested listening for melody:

English folk song – "Fantasia on Greensleeves" by Ralph Vaughan Williams

Music is further enhanced with the addition of harmony. **Harmony** is created when tones are combined and sound simultaneously. These tones are usually arranged in a manner that produces sounds that are pleasing to the ear. Harmonic sounds are typically written to complement each other and provide structure within the music. How to construct harmony is of its own study, however, it is important for every musician to understand the relationship between melody and harmony. A harmony cannot exist without a melody, but melody can exist without a harmony.

Suggested listening for harmony:

Rock – "I Get Around" by The Beach Boys

Whenever two tones are written to simultaneously occur, this is called a **chord**. Harmony is usually structured with chords. Two of the most popular instruments in modern music, the piano and the guitar, use chords frequently. Some instruments cannot play a chord alone, such as woodwinds and brass instruments, because they can only produce a single tone at a time. The sounds of these instruments can be a part of a chord, however, when combined with additional instruments in an arrangement of music.

A basic and common form of chords found in music is the **triad**. A triad implies three notes or tones, sounding simultaneously. On the musical staff, a triad will appear as a neat stack of three notes.

These three triads are all in root position. **Root position** refers to how the three notes are stacked. The **root** of a chord is the "home note" of the chord. A triad is named after its root. In the images below are C major triads in each of the four clefs we've studied. The note "C" is the bottom of each triad.

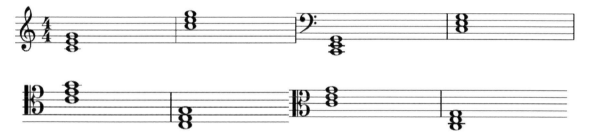

The three notes of a triad are the first, third, and fifth notes of a scale. In a C Major scale, "C", "E", and "G" are the root, 3rd, and 5th notes. Any triad containing these three notes is a C Major triad or chord. To construct an A Minor triad, the notes "A", "C", and "E" would be used because they are the root, 3rd, and 5th notes of the A Minor scale.

The notes of a triad can be arranged in a different order on the staff using the same three notes. For example, in a C Major triad, "E" or "G" could be written as the bottom note instead. This is called a **chord inversion**. Pianists will study this more in depth, as well as anyone pursuing music theory. For the purposes of this guide, we are going to focus on basic major and minor triads.

Exercise 14.1

Construct the major or minor triad for each of the following major and minor scales by determining the root, 3rd, and 5th notes of each scale. Write the triad as letter names. For example, your answer could read "C Major Triad - C, E, G". Write your answers on a sheet of paper to check with on page 141.

Major Scales	Minor Scales
A B C# D E F# G# A	*C D Eb F G Ab Bb C*
Bb C D Eb F G A Bb	*D E F G A Bb C D*
F G A Bb C D E F	*F# G# A B C# D E F#*

Sometimes in sheet music, you may see uppercase letters above some of the measures. These uppercase letters are **chord symbols,** and depending on the instrument you play, may be a playable part for you. For major triads, an uppercase letter is used. So, a C Major triad may be notated with an uppercase "C". For minor triads, an uppercase letter is used followed by a lowercase "m". An "A" Minor triad would be written as "Am".

A sheet of music like the example above is called a **lead sheet**. This type of music notes the melody on the staff and includes the harmony as chord symbols written above the measures. Lead sheets are common in jazz ensemble playing to allow for creative freedom amongst the musicians. The lead sheet establishes some structure to abide by, but leaves freedom for individualism in how the notes of each chord might be arranged and timed within the meter.

Exercise 14.2

The image below is a musical line from a lead sheet. For each chord symbol, identify the three notes needed to create that triad. Be sure to check if there is a lowercase "m" indicating that the triad is minor. Use the formula for the major and minor scales found on page 75 to help with determining the root, 3rd, and 5th notes of the affiliated scale for the answer. Check your answers on page 141.

Congratulations on reaching the end of Week 2! In Days 8–14 this week, you learned about pitch, the music alphabet, the staff, clefs, accidentals, intervals, scales, key signatures, melody, harmony, and chords. You now have an understanding of two of the most essential elements in music: rhythm from Week 1 and pitch from Week 2. Revisit any lesson completed this far as needed to keep your knowledge of these studies sharp.

Week 2 Highlights

- Pitch is the frequency-based scale relating how high and low a sound is heard.
- Notes are the written form of pitches in respect to the frequency and duration.
- The first seven letters of the English alphabet, "A-B-C-D-E-F-G", are used to classify pitches. Notes of the same pitch class are discerned using register numbers, starting with "A0", "B0", "C1", etc.
- The staff is the five lines and four spaces where music is notated. The separate lines and spaces are places for note heads to be written.
- Pitch is written as notes on a staff that reflect the pitch class and register in relation to the clef and which line or space to which the note belongs.
- The two most common clefs are treble clef and bass clef. When joined together with a brace, these clefs create the grand staff.
- Alto and tenor clef are the two C Clefs that are used in modern music.
- A half step is the distance between two consecutive pitches and notes.
- Sharps raise a pitch by a half step. Flats lower a pitch by a half step. Naturals cancel out a sharp or flat. Sharps, flats, and naturals are collectively called accidentals.
- Intervals are the measurement of distance between two consecutive or simultaneous notes.
- An octave is the interval of an 8th. Octaves are frequently found in music.
- 8va indicates to play a note or passage of notes one octave higher or lower depending on if the indicator is above or below the staff. 8vb indicates to play the notes an octave lower.
- Scales are a sequence of pitches or notes organized within an octave. The specific ordering of half steps and whole steps can create major and minor scales.
- Major and minor scales are the foundations of the key. In music, the key is what scale the music is centered around, especially in relation to the "home note", or first note of the scale.
- A key signature is found at the beginning of each line of music and notifies the musician of what notes might be flat or sharp throughout the music following the key signature.
- There is a major and minor key for each pitch class, which would be twelve in total when including all notes possible within an octave.

- Melody is the primary line in music. Harmony can be added with simultaneous notes, and is often arranged into a chordal structure.
- Triads are chords that contain three notes and are extremely common in music that includes harmony. The three notes are the root, 3rd, and 5th note of a major or minor scale. Triads can be major or minor.
- Chord symbols are sometimes found above measures of music as uppercase letters or uppercase letters with a lowercase "m" attached to indicate a minor triad.
- Lead sheets have the melody notated on a staff with chord symbols above measures within that chordal structure.

Week 3 - Expressive Elements of Music

This week will involve the exploration of the more abstract side of music, expression. The first two weeks focused on rhythm and pitch, which contains tangible, quantifiable, and objective content. The expressive elements of music are less concrete; they are influenced by personal tastes, opinions, and interpretations. While there are performance practices and impartial markings and terms, the element of expression should involve interpretation. Composers indicate guidelines to their interpretive intentions through the markings and terms we will examine today. The performance of these markings is influenced by the composer, the style of the time period the music was written, and the performer's personal interpretation.

There are innumerous words and ways to express mood and emotions. This week's content will include the most common and most essential to get you started. It is advisable for future reference to have a reliable resource to consult with when an unknown symbol or term occurs. Many musicians own musical dictionaries and/or thesauruses to use for quick reference should the occasion arise that they were to come across an unfamiliar word, term, or symbol. While this guide will include dozens of terms and symbols throughout and in the glossary at the end, there are more out there yet that you may discover in a piece of music. There are also several legitimate online resources to use for future reference.

A majority of the terminology and abbreviations we will analyze today are in Italian. Italy was an epicenter of musical innovation and development at the time that music notation started to become standardized. So, it is standard and tradition to use the established Italian terms and abbreviations. Remember that these terms and definitions will be listed in the glossary for quick reference. *Andiamo!*

Day 15 – Dynamics

Music can be played at various levels of volume. The loudness or softness of music is organized and notated using symbols called **dynamics**. Dynamic markings are guides for the volume level of a section to be played. The degrees of loudness implied from these markings are relative to each other and the character of the music. There is not a set level for any marking because they are dependent on the performer's interpretation of the dynamic relationships. There are some guidelines.

From the Italian to the English language, the word *forte* translates to loud. The word *piano* translates to soft. These are the two most basic dynamic indications found in music, abbreviated with their first letter; "*p*" for piano and "*f*" for forte. Dynamic markings are abbreviations from the Italian terminology. It is widely accepted to learn the Italian terms because music from around the world uses these same symbols and terms.

When used in music, the dynamic marking will often be notated beneath the note or notes to which the dynamic applies. In some music. dynamic marks can be found above the note or notes to which it applies, and on the grand staff, the marking will be between the two staves. The dynamic marking continues to apply to all subsequent notes until the next dynamic marking occurs. The musical line in the example directly above would be played *forte* from the start until the performer reaches measure five, where the dynamic changes to *piano*.

Exercise 15.1

Rehearse the exercise below by clapping, tapping, or vocalizing the rhythm. Notice that there are dynamic markings added to indicate loudness or softness.

More subtle degrees of volume are indicated with the addition of the prefixes **Mezzo** and **più.** Mezzo translates to "moderately", and is used in conjunction with forte or piano. *Mezzo forte* (mf) indicates "moderately loud" and *mezzo piano* (*mp*) indicates "moderately soft". The addition of *più* indicates "more loud" or "more soft"; for example, *più forte* or *più piano* respectively.

The *p* and *f* symbols are commonly doubled to expand their meanings. The marking *pp* would read *pianissimo*, meaning "very soft". With the *f* sign, *ff* is read *fortissimo*, "very loud". In Italian, the suffix "*-issimo*" adds extra emphasis to the meaning of the attached word.

Suggested listening for loud vs. soft dynamics:

Classical – "In the Hall of the Mountain King" by Edvard Grieg

Exercise 15.2

In the line below, the same rhythmic sequence is used in each measure with varying dynamic markings. Practice these measures observing the dynamic markings.

Gradual change in volumes is also possible on most instruments. The symbols for these gradual changes are line forms called **crescendo**, **decrescendo**, and **diminuendo**.

A crescendo indicates to gradually get louder. Its symbol goes from small to large space between the lines to reflect the increase in volume. In music, sometimes the abbreviate *cresc.* is written rather than the symbol. The opposite of a crescendo is a decrescendo. This symbol has a larger space between the lines and gets smaller to reflect the decrease of the volume. It is sometimes abbreviated as *decresc.* A diminuendo symbol is the same as a decrescendo symbol, and can be abbreviated dim.

cresc. _ _ _ _ _   dim. _ _ _ _ _ _ _

Suggested listening for gradual dynamic changes:

<u>Ballet</u> – " Theme from Swan Lake" by Pyotr Ilyich Tchaikovsky

Exercise 15.3

The rhythm line below features quarter notes with crescendo and decrescendo. Rehearse this line to gain proficiency in gradually increasing and decreasing the dynamic level. The highest point of the crescendo should occur on the note marked forte. This is referred to as the peak of the crescendo.

There are terms that can be added to the abbreviations or words for the gradual changes. **Poco** is "little" in English, and might be seen with *cresc.* as *poco cresc,* meaning to get a little louder. **Poco a poco** means "little by little", and when combined with crescendo would indicate to "get louder, little by little", implying a longer duration of increasing volume.

Dynamics can also change suddenly rather than gradually. To indicate this, the word **subito** is used. This word translates to "suddenly", and is often abbreviated as **s** or **sub.** A marking of **subito piano,** abbreviated *sub p* or **sp** would be placed where the music would get soft suddenly. A special dynamic marking called **forte-piano** is used to indicate a note or passage that begins loudly, forte, and then immediately drops to soft, or piano.

sub p   *sub f*   *fp*

Suggested listening for sudden dynamic changes:

<u>Classical</u> – "Symphony No. 94: Mvmt. 2" by Joseph Haydn

There is existing music that goes beyond these parameters of dynamics and cross into extreme dynamics. These are markings like "*ppp*" or "*fff*" and sometimes composers go further adding more "p's" or "f's" to push the limits. Remember that dynamics are not concrete levels of volume and are in relation to each other, and also take into account the intended character and interpretation of the music.

Suggested listening for extreme dynamics:

<u>Classical</u> – "The Planets - Movement Mars" by Gustav Holst

There are additional terms that are used in reference to overall dynamic changes. **Smorzando** means to "smother the dynamic to nothing." **Espressivo** can be interpreted to add loudness and softness for contrast in order to emote throughout the musical line. Espressivo gives the performer creative freedom to follow the character and intuition of the musical line to add dynamic fluctuations, and even tempo fluctuations when appropriate.

Day 16 - Style & Articulation

Along with dynamic markings of loudness and softness, there are markings that indicate how a note is attacked, or approached in performance. How a note is approached or attacked is called the **articulation.** Notes can be articulated strongly, gently, loudly, softly, smoothly, detached, and combinations of all. There are specific markings that indicate the desired articulation.

A **slur** is a curved line connecting pitches of different classes. <u>The notes must be changing within the slur, otherwise the curved line would function like a tie.</u> Slurs can be short, between two notes, or they can be entire musical passages. Any notes located within the slurred passage would be played smoothly, without any break in the sound. This is achieved with techniques specific to each instrument. The desired sound is a smooth, connected, flowing sound for notes within a slur. This style of music is called **legato,** which is Italian for "smooth, connected."

Slurs can connect any number of notes granted they are in succession and not the exact same pitch. In the example above, there are slurred notes in groups of two, three four, and even a multi-measure slur.

Exercise 16.1

In the musical line below, identify if each curved line is a slur or a tie. Answers are found from left to right on page 142 of the answer key.

A similar style to slurs, **tenuto** markings indicate to play the note to its fullest value. The marking is a single, short horizontal line notated above or below the note. Similar to a slur, the notes will be smooth and connected, but unlike a slur, there will also be a minimal amount of separation and a clear start or attack to each note. In jazz, the sound of this articulation is conceptualized with the word "doo".

Tenuto

The opposite of legato is ***staccato***. A staccato marking is a small, single dot written above or below the note head. It will never be next to the note head, because dots to the right of the note head add duration as we learned back in Week 1. The staccato dot indicates that the note to be played detached, or separated. If quantified, a staccato-quarter note would sound the duration of an eighth note followed by an eighth rest. Jazz uses the word "dit" to resemble the sound of staccato.

Staccato

An additional marking used to signify extreme separation between notes is the ***staccatissimo.*** This is an elongated dot with a point that is interpreted as being shorter than staccato, however composers in the classical era and prior would use the two interchangeably. A staccatissimo quarter note would sound the duration of a sixteenth note followed by rests for the remainder of the beat.

Staccatissimo

Suggested listening for staccato vs. legato:

<u>Classical</u> – "Symphony No. 6: Mvmt 2" by Ludwig Van Beethoven

Exercise 16.2

The musical line below contains staccato dots and rhythmic dots that add duration. Determine how many of each by distinguishing the placement of the dots. Check your answers on page 142.

When a composer wishes to indicate emphasis on a particular note, set of notes, or chord, an **accent** is used. This marking is identical to the "greater than" sign used in mathematics. It indicates to play the notes it is attached to strongly, with stress and emphasis. Jazz practice uses "dah" to represent accent.

Accent

In the same vein, *marcato* markings are also used to indicate the note be played strongly. With a marcato, the interpretation is more forceful and louder than an accent. In notation, the marcato mark is almost always above the staff regardless of the direction of the stem of the note it affects. "Daht" is said in jazz for the sound of marcato.

Marcato

Suggested listening for marcato and accent:

Classical – "Symphony No. 9: Mvmt. 4" by Antonin Dvořák

Exercise 16.3

Count how many marcato vs. accent marks are used in the musical line below. Write down your answers and check on page 142 for accuracy.

There are additional markings used to create emphasis in music along with accent and marcato markings. A ***sforzando,*** abbreviated ***sfz,*** is a marking that indicates sudden emphasis, or a forceful accent. ***Forzando,*** abbreviated ***fz,*** indicates the same expression. The degree of emphasis depends on the dynamic level and context of the music and is open to the performer's interpretation.

Sforzando and Forzando

All of the articulation markings above can stand alone or be used in combination with each other. For example, an accent and tenuto marking can be paired to create an emphasized, full length note.

The articulation markings so far have indicated how to approach a specified note or group of notes. Stylistic expressions can also be found in music to indicate the mood of a passage of notes. There are dozens of options, and we will mention a few of the most common.

Music marked as ***dolce*** would be played delicately, and likely on the softer side of dynamics, because dolce translates to "sweetly". ***Cantabile*** translates to "singable, songlike". Music marked cantabile might be performed in a smooth, lyrical manner that aims to imitate the human voice. In contrast, ***agitato*** translates to "agitated". This may imply to play more loudly and sometimes quicken the tempo, or speed. ***Ad libitum,*** translation "with free rhythm and expression", gives the performer freedom with music marked ad libitum or *ad lib* for short. This may include dynamic and tempo fluctuations that the player or singer finds appealing.

Mood markings such as the four just mentioned are notated under or above the note or notes which it begins to apply. Like dynamic markings, these expressions apply to the subsequent passage of notes until a new marking or section of music begins.

In the example above, dolce is marked at the beginning, which would imply a lighter, softer sound and approach. At measure 4, cantabile is added which would imply to play or sing out more fully, imitative of a singer. There are countless descriptive words in Italian and any language used to denote style.

Day 17 - Tempo Markings

Back in Week 1, we discussed tempo markings found as Beats Per Minute, or BPM. BPM are numerical measurements of tempo that a metronome can be set to make audible the speed of the pulse. Tempo markings do not necessarily have to be marked in BPM and are not always measured using a number. There are expressive terms and markings that can be used to imply the tempo, sometimes with the addition of mood implications. For example, yesterday, we discussed the *agitato* marking. Agitato implies to quicken the pace of the music as well as approach the music in an agitated manner. Let's begin our study today with six of the most prolific Italian terms used to indicate tempo.

The slowest of the six we will mention today is ***Largo.*** Largo is Italian for "wide, or broad", and indicates a very slow tempo. On a metronome, Largo can be set anywhere between 40-60 BPM.

Suggested listening for Largo tempo:

Classical – "Symphony No. 9: Mvmt 2" by Antonin Dvořák

Adagio is Italian for "slowly, at ease" and is more literal with its implication. Adagio is not quite as slow as Largo, and would be 66-76 BPM.

Suggested listening for Adagio tempo:

Classical – "Adagio for Strings" by Samuel Barber

The next tempo of our six in order of quickness is ***Andante.*** In Italian, andante means "walking". This tempo marking is slightly ambiguous and is often described as "at a walking pace". It is faster than adagio with a metronomic setting of 76-108 BPM.

Suggested listening for Andante tempo:

<u>Classical</u> – "Piano Concerto No. 21: Mvmt 2" by Wolfgang Amadeus Mozart

Perhaps the simplest to memorize, **Moderato** translates to "moderately". This "moderate" tempo marking is like the middle of our tempos at 98-112 BPM.

Suggested listening for Moderato tempo:

<u>Classical</u> – "Piano Concerto No. 2: Mvmt. 1" by Sergei Rachmaninoff

Allegro directly translates to "cheerful" from Italian. In music, it is described as a "bright, brisk, or fast tempo". Its BPM is between 120-156 BPM.

Suggested listening for Allegro tempo:

<u>Classical</u> – "Symphony No. 5: Mvmt 1" by Ludwig Van Beethoven

The final of the six basic tempo markings is **Presto.** The literal translation of presto is "soon". In music, presto is a very, very fast tempo. The BPM for presto is 168-200 BPM.

Suggested listening for Presto tempo:

<u>Classical</u> – "Concerto No. 2 in G minor: Summer" by Antonio Vivaldi

Exercise 17.1

So far, we have discussed six tempo markings. Each is listed in the table below. Set your metronome to a number of each range and tap along with the rate of each tempo.

Largo	40-60 BPM
Adagio	66-76 BPM
Andante	76-108 BPM
Moderato	98-112 BPM
Allegro	120-156 BPM
Presto	168-200 BPM

You may have noticed that there are gaps between some of the BPM ranges between tempos. One way this is addressed is with the use of Italian suffixes in addition to the tempo markings above. The suffix *"-issimo"* indicates an exaggeration of the attached tempo. In Italian, this suffix can be attached to just about any adjective to form the "absolute superlative" of that word. **Larghissimo** is the slowest tempo marking possible, with any BPM of 24 or less.

An additional suffix commonly used with tempo markings is "*-etto*". This suffix means "little". **Allegretto** means "a little fast" and is slightly slower than Allegro at 102-110 BPM. A third Italian suffix used in tempo markings is "*-tino*", which translates to "little" as well. It is used with andante as **andantino.** Andantino is another ambiguous term that has changed interpretations. Currently, it is interpreted as "a little faster than andante" at 80-108 BPM.

In music from the Baroque, Classical, Romantic eras of music, the titles of pieces and movements were the tempo markings of the musical work or movement. It was incredibly common to name a piece of music something like "Adagio in F Major", reflective of the key and tempo of the music.

Beyond the concrete tempo markings that establish a tempo for a piece of music, there are additional markings that indicate fluctuations of tempo. These markings indicate for the tempo to change gradually, and sometimes temporarily.

Ritardando translates to "delaying" and is used in music to gradually slow the tempo. It is often abbreviated as **rit.** or **ritard.** Notes above a ritardando should become increasingly delayed until the end of the ritardando is notated. This can be indicated with a dashed line or with either the marking *a tempo* (a tempo is pronounced "ah" tempo) or *tempo primo,* which translates to "first time." Both tempo primo and a tempo directs to return to the previous tempo that was marked before the fluctuation.

An additional term that is musically synonymous with ritardando is **rallentando,** which translates to "slowing down." A rallentando functions the same as a ritardando, which is to gradually slow down.

Meno mosso is an additional way to express for the music to slow down, but it doesn't imply gradually. Its literal translation is "less motion", and music marked **meno mosso** should be played more slowly than the previous passage.

Exercise 17.2

In the rhythm line below, there is a ritardando indicated at the sixth measure that lasts until the end of the line. Clap, tap, or vocalize this line starting with a steady, moderate tempo until the ritardando is reached. At that point, gradually slow the tempo until the end of the line. Because of the tempo fluctuation, do not use a metronome.

ritard.

While ritardando, rallentando, and meno mosso are indications of the tempo getting gradually slower, **accelerando** indicates the opposite. Accelerando translates to "accelerating", and its implication in music is to do just that. A passage marked with accelerando should gradually increase in speed until otherwise noted. This could be until the end of a piece or a new marking that differs appears such as a new tempo marking.

Exercise 17.3

The musical line below features an accelerando starting in measure 4 and continuing to the end of the line. Clap, tap, or vocalize the line starting at a slow steady tempo. Stay steady until measure four and then incrementally begin picking up speed. Try to be gradual, saving the fastest for the final few notes. The beginnings of each measure are accented, so give extra emphasis to these notes along the way. Because of the tempo fluctuation, do not use a metronome for this exercise.

accelerando...

Suggested listening for accelerando:

<u>Classical</u> – "The Sailor's Hornpipe" by Henry Woods

Two special symbols to mention today don't directly change the speed or tempo of the music. These markings "stop time" in two different approaches. A ***fermata*** (sometimes called a bird's eye) is a symbol written above or below a note or chord that indicates for that note or chord to be sustained for longer than its usual duration. The duration is unspecified and is in the hands of the conductor or performer to interpret how long is appropriate to the musical line. The image of the symbol is pictured below.

Fermata

The second symbol that stops time is the ***caesura.*** This marking appears as two diagonal lines at the top of the staff. A caesura directs the performer or ensemble to completely stop. It's as if the music were paused for a short duration. This can be used as a sudden, or dramatic effect in a composition.

Caesura

Exercise 17.4

For this exercise, clap, tap, or vocalize the line below, observing the fermatas and caesura along the way. Notice that a fermata may be printed above or below the staff.

The final tempo related marking to discuss today involves an abundance of interpretive involvement. ***Rubato*** is derived from the Italian word for "to rob". In musical terms, it is defined as "stolen time". It is used to allow rhythmic and expressive freedom of the tempo at the discretion of the musician. Music marked rubato can be sped up and slowed down nearly at will. It is common practice to give back the time you "rob". Basically, the time you take, you return, meaning that if you slow down one part, speed up another to even out the give and take of the tempo.

Suggested listening for rubato style:

Classical – "Prelude in E Minor" by Frédéric Chopin

There are even more Italian terms used to express tempo beyond what we examined today. Tempo markings can be also found in other languages. Italian has become universally standard for expressive markings like tempo, articulation, and dynamics, but there are composers that opt to use their native language instead. In your music studies, you may come across terms from languages from around the world.

Day 18 - Straight vs. Swing

Today's focus is a marking related to rhythm. Before we dive in, let's do a quick review of a few pertinent rhythmic elements of eighth notes. Recall that back in Week 1, we learned that eighth notes are the division of a quarter note and are the duration of 1/8 of a whole note. In most time signatures, this is half of a beat. They are often paired together to complete a beat and beamed together to reflect their beat groupings.

When we were practicing eighth notes during Week 1, the eighth notes were always an even division of the beat. Two eighth notes would sound equally in duration within a single beat. These are specifically **straight eighths**, which is the default in music. However, there is a marking that changes all of this. The style of music that changes our eighth-note concepts is **swing.**

Swing music uses a new system of counting eighth notes, called **swing eighths.** Swing eighths are still a division of a single beat, but the two sounds are not evenly distributed. In any time signature in swing music, a quarter-note division into two eighth notes remains constant. What is different is how the eighth notes are counted and performed. Of a pair of eighth notes sharing a single beat, the first eighth note receives slightly more of the beat than the second. This creates the laid back, casual feeling of swing that is easiest to pick-up through listening.

Initially, it is easier to feel swing than it is to count it. To count it, it is best to equate the pattern with an existing rhythm. On the left of the equal sign is two eighth notes, and on the right is the alteration required to create swing eighths.

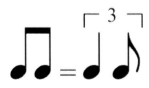

Oftentimes, swing eighths are counted thinking "1-ah-2-ah-3-ah-4-ah" with the second division of each beat being on the relaxed side in a triplet feel. It is counted and felt as if the beat were divided into triplet-eighth notes, and the first two have been tied together.

Exercise 18.1

The line of rhythm below will train you how to feel the swing eighths. Start with the metronome set to 60 BPM. Notice that the third measure ties the first two eighth notes of each triplet, and that the last measure is the same exact rhythm written without the tie. This means they are counted and should sound the exact same. The final measure is how swing eighth notes are equated.

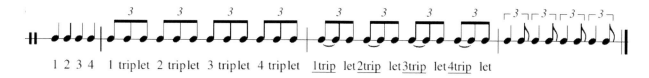

Exercise 18.2

This line of music begins with the expression "swing". Eighth-note pairs will sound like each beat of the last measure of exercise 18.3. Practice the following line with the metronome set to 60-70 BPM. Once proficient at slower tempos, feel free to increase the speed for challenge.

The word swing can be found at the beginning of the musical composition and can apply to the entirety of the piece. It can also be used for passages of music and will be written above the measure that begins the swing-style section. If a song were to switch back to straight eighth after swinging, the word "straight" or words "straight eighths" would be at the end of the swung passage.

Exercise 18.3

In order to count, tap, or vocalize the following line accurately, you will need to be prepared to switch from swing-eighth-note feel to straight-eighth notes in the last two measures. It may be helpful to rehearse the sections separately with a metronome before putting it together in one cohesive line. Remember to start slow until you are ready to speed up the tempo.

Musicians that hope to learn to play and/or sing in the jazz style will need to build proficiency with feeling and performing in swing style. An ample quantity of music from the 1930's and 1940's was written in the swing style. You may even recognize some of the listening examples from the Swing Era listed below.

Suggested listening for Swing Era:

"It Don't Mean a Thing, If You Ain't Got That Swing" by Duke Ellington
"In the Mood" by Glenn Miller
"Sing, Sing, Sing" by Benny Goodman

Day 19 - Musical Navigation

The general structure of music notation was discussed at the beginning of this guide. You learned that bar lines organize the music into measures, and these measures are organized into beats that are determined by the meter, or time signature. We also examined double bar lines, which end a song, and repeat signs, which lead us back to a spot in the music to play again. Today we will add extensions to the musical structure that's established.

Let's begin by expanding upon ways to use the repeat sign. The uses, discussed back in Week 1, are still viable. But, there are a few signs that may be notated in the music along with the repeat sign. These additions are brackets called **volta brackets,** and they are used when an excerpt of the music is to be played again (repeated), but has different endings to each repeat. These bracketed endings can be used for a single repeat or for multiple repeats, and the number of volta brackets will likely correspond with the number of repeats.

When reading music with these brackets, the specific volta bracket is named after its number as an "**ending**". A volta bracket with the number one in it would be called the "first ending", the number two would be the "second ending", etc. In the examples above, the top line of music has two endings, and the bottom line of music has three. When repeating a passage with volta brackets, each ending is only played once. This means that on the repeat, the first ending will not be played again. It will be skipped over for the second ending, since this is the second time through the passage. Let's apply this to the volta example from above with three endings.

In this line, the measures are numbered consecutively, 1 through 8. Abiding by the repeats and volta brackets, the measures would be performed in the following order: 1-2-3-4-5-6; 1-2-3-4-5-7; 1-2-3-4-5-8.

Exercise 19.1

For the musical example below, determine the order the measures would be performed. The measures are numbered 1 through 9. Write your answers on a sheet of paper and check them with the answer key on page 142.

While it is common for the endings to be found at the conclusion of a piece of music, volta brackets are not exclusively at the end. They can occur anywhere within a piece of music and will function in the same manner. Also, endings can be multi-measure.

Exercise 19.2

The repeat structure in this example is more extensive. The measures are lettered below. Determine the order in which this line would occur, observing the repeat signs and volta brackets. Write your answer using the letters below each measure and check them on page 142.

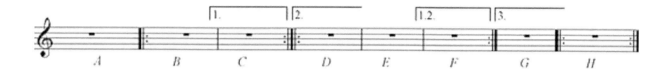

The following symbols and terms are part of a system of signs that direct the musician with jumps in the music that do not involve repeat signs. First, let's start with the marking *fine.* Although it uses the same letters as the English word, fine, this word is Italian and is pronounced "fee-nay". *Fine* translates to "end", and the same definition is used in music. It is not used for just any ordinary ending however, that is why the double bar line is used. *Fine* is used in conjunction with either ***da capo,*** abbreviated **D.C.**, or ***dal segno,*** abbreviated **D.S.**

Da capo translates to "from the head", and in music directs the musician to start playing "from the beginning". In music it is usually abbreviated *D.C.* and indicates at that point in the music, to jump back to the beginning and play to the end. Da capo will often be paired with a direction for where to play to after the jump to the beginning. **D.C. al Fine** indicates to, at that point in the music, jump back to the beginning, and play from there until the *Fine* sign.

In the top example below, the D.C at the end of measure six directs the musician to jump back to the beginning at that point, and then play through the line to the end. This means you would not play the last measure until after jumping back and playing the preceding measures again.

This next example features the D.C paired with Fine. In this musical line, the performer would play from the beginning to the end of the line, jump back to the beginning, but this time play to the fine at the end of measure four.

The *segno* is a specific sign used in music to mark a jump, and segno appropriately translates to the word sign. This sign is used with the navigational phrase dal segno, which literally translates to "from the sign".

Segno

In music, **dal segno, or D.S.,** indicates to jump back to the sign symbol shown above, or the segno. In the musical line directly below, the measures are lettered to clarify. To play this line accurately observing the D.S. structure, the musician would play the measures in the following order: A, B, C, D, E, F, G, B, C, D, E, F, G, H, I.

Dal segno systems are often paired with a direction, similar to da capo. For example, **D.S. al fine** would instruct the musician to, at that point in the music, jump back to the segno and then play from there until the fine. Below is the same musical line as the previous example, but with a fine added. The sequence of the line in measure letters would be A, B, C, D, E, F, G, H, I, B, C, D.

Exercise 19.3

For this exercise, write down the order of the measures using the letters found below. Be certain to follow any signs or indications of jumps. Check your answers with page 142 of the answer key.

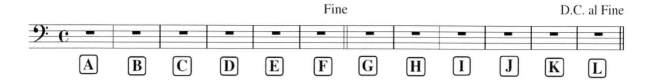

Fine   D.C. al Fine

A B C D E F G H I J K L

Exercise 19.4

The following line of music has indications of jumps in the music. List the order the measures should be performed using the letters below each measure. On a sheet of paper, write your answers and check with page 143.

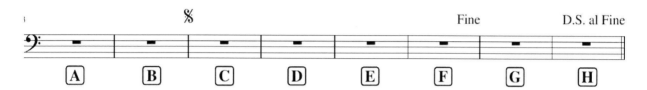

A B C D E F G H

The final road map term and symbol that is used with the dal segno and da capo markings is the *coda.* From Italian, *coda* translates to "tail", and in music is used to label the ending excerpt of the music. The word coda or the coda symbol may be used to indicate where the ending section begins. The direction from where to jump to the coda is signified sometimes with the phrase "to coda" or with the coda symbol pictured below (often called a bull's eye).

Coda

The coda symbol will be found at the point in the music where the musician should jump to the coda, or the end. This occurs after either a jump to the beginning (da capo), or a jump to the sign (dal segno). **D.C. al Coda** would mean that at that point in the music, jump to the beginning, play until the coda sign, and then jump to the coda. **D.S. al Coda** would direct the musician to, at that point in the music, jump to the segno, play until the coda sign, and then jump to the coda.

The excerpt of music below demonstrates the D.C. al Coda structure. The musician would play from the beginning to the D.C. al Coda text, jump back the beginning, play until the To Coda text, and then jump to the coda sign on the final line of music.

The excerpt of music below demonstrates the D.S. al Coda structure. The musician would begin from the top, play until the D.S. al Coda text, jump to the segno, play until the "to coda" text, and then jump to the coda sign on the last line to play to the end.

Exercise 19.5

This exercise practices sequencing the jumps of a D.C. al Coda structure. On a sheet of paper, write the order of the lettered measures. Check your answers with page 143 of the answer key.

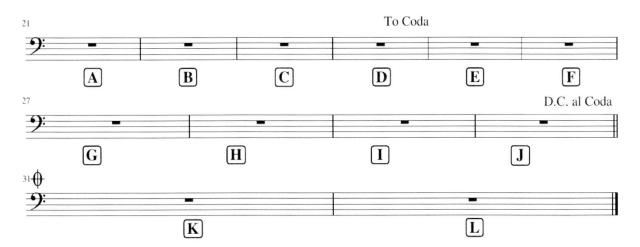

Exercise 19.6

This exercise practices the jumps of the D.S. al Coda structure. Write the letters in the order in which they would occur according to the signs and symbols above the staff. Check your answers with page 143.

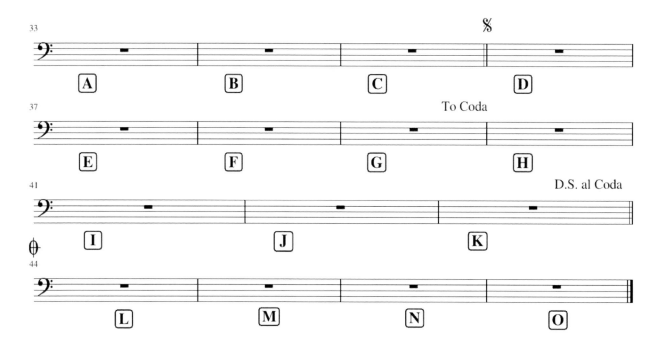

Day 20 – Ornaments

Ornaments are embellishments that may be added into the music using the symbols examined today. These markings are not essential to the musical line, but they add variety and interest. Ornaments are added notes that decorate the music. Sometimes these added notes are printed in particular ways, and other times they are implied by a symbol.

Trills are marked above a note as a **tr** or **tr~** depending on the length of the trill. To perform a trill, the note the symbol is printed above or below is rapidly alternated with the note one higher than the printed note. It is possible for the higher trilled note to be a half step or a whole step above the printed note. This is determined usually by the key signature, but can be altered with the addition of an accidental along with the trill indication.

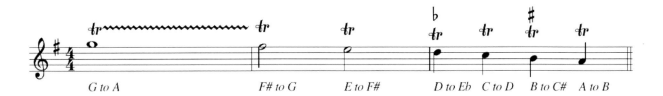

| G to A | | F# to G | E to F# | D to Eb | C to D | B to C# | A to B |

Let's examine the trills in the musical example above. Beneath each note are the letter names of the note printed in the treble clef followed by the note to which the player would trill. Notice that the second note is F# sharp because of the key signature, and the third note, E, trills up to F# because of the key signature. There is an example of a trill with a flat and one with a sharp added to indicate an accidental outside of the key signature that alters the trill.

Exercise 20.1

The letters below represent notes on a staff in the key of D Major. Determine what note these notes would trill to by identifying what note would be one step above the lettered note. The key signature is printed in each clef studied for reference. Write your answers and consult with page 143.

tr tr tr tr tr tr tr
D E F# G A B C#

117

Depending on the style and time period of the music the trill is found, sometimes it is performance practice to start the trill on the upper tone. For example, the note "C" could trill up to "D", and in baroque music it is assumed to begin the trill on "D".

The **mordent** is similar to a trill, but much shorter in duration. A mordent begins with the printed note, rapidly changes to the note below that note, and then returns to the original printed note. This type of mordent is also called the lower mordent because it steps down. An upper mordent, or inverted mordent is the other way around.

 In the image to the left of this text, the first note is a "D" with an upper mordent marking above it. The second note is a "C" with a lower mordent marking above it. The latter is distinguished from the former with a vertical line through the middle of the undulant line. The first upper mordent on "D" indicates to play "D-E-D" in rapid succession. The second lower mordent on "C" would be played "C-B-C" in rapid succession. Like trills, mordents of either type adhere to the key signature unless modified by a flat, sharp, or natural sign.

Exercise 20.2

The following treble clef notes have either an upper or lower mordent marking. For each note, determine which way the added note will step (up or down), and what note to which it would alternate. The letter names of each note are printed below the staff. After checking the key signature, on a sheet of paper write the names of the note alterations. Check your answers on page 144.

The **turn** in music is a symbol that represents multiple-note additions. It is an s-shaped symbol that is notated above the staff either directly above a note or above the space between consecutive notes. The shape of the curve indicates the directions of the notes. Tracing the "S" from left to right, it flows from center-up-center-down-center, with center being the original note printed on the staff. In the image below, the S-sign is demonstrating a turn indicated on the note "C".

Turn

The S-sign can be inverted to create an inverted turn. Following the curves of the inverted S, the direction of the notes would be center-down-center-up-center. This is the inverse of the regular turn previously analyzed.

Inverted Turn

Exercise 20.3

The following notes are in bass clef. Find the two notes with the s-sign indicating a turn or inverted turn in the music. Using the letter name printed below the staff and the key signature, write the letter names of the notes that would occur for each turn. Include the printed note appropriately by listing the pitches in order from left to right as they would occur. Check your answer on page 144.

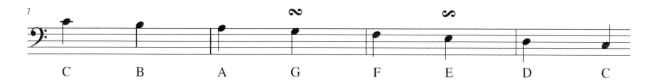

Ornaments can also take the form of miniature notes preceding a regularly printed note. These are most often a **grace note**. Grace notes appear on the staff as miniature notes before a regularly printed note, referred to as the principal note. These can appear as a single little note or can be multiple notes grouped together. How they are played depends on historical context in the music and a small distinguishing mark.

A single grace note with an oblique slash through the stem indicates the intention of an **acciaccatura.** This type of grace note is not emphasized compared to the principal note to which it is attached. The grace note is often one step above or below the principal note, but it can be higher or lower, or there can even be multiple grace notes grouped to one principal note. An acciaccatura is to be played very quickly either immediately on or before the beat. The placement is dependent upon the performance practice based on the time period that the music was written and who wrote it.

The image above are examples of acciaccatura grace notes. Grace notes can be higher or lower than the principal note, may have accidentals, and appear in multi-note groups. When in a group, the oblique slash may be through only the initial grace note, as pictured on the far right.

When the grace note does not have an oblique slash through the stem, it serves as an **appoggiatura**. While the acciaccatura is played quickly with emphasis on the principal note, an appoggiatura is melodically important and receives emphasis. It most often receives half the value of the principal note.

An appoggiatura grace note can be higher or lower than the principal note, and can also appear in groups and with accidentals.

Exercise 20.4

For each measure below, determine if the grace note is an acciaccatura or an appoggiatura. Remember to check the stem for any oblique slashes. You can check your answers with the key on page 144.

Perhaps the ornament found in music that is the most pleasing to perform is the **glissando.** Indicated with a long line between two notes, a glissando sounds like a musical slide. The line is sometimes wavy or straight, but the definition remains consistent. Every note between the two primary pitches is to be sounded in quick, slurred succession, creating a sliding effect. Glissandi can go up or down and are used between notes of various durations.

An ornament marking related to the trill is the **tremolo.** This embellishment creates a trembling effect in the music. There are two different ways a tremolo is observed. One is the rapid reiteration of a single note, and the other is a rapid alteration of two different notes. The latter sounds similar to a trill, and it is, but there is one distinguishing factor. A trill is between two adjacent notes, while a tremolo is between two notes that are further apart. On some instruments, such as the piano, a tremolo can indicate rapid alternation between two chords.

In the image above, these slashed lines below the whole note and on the stems of the half and quarter notes indicates a tremolo. This type of tremolo would be performed by rapidly repeating the indicated note. How quickly is indicated by the number of lines in the tremolo.

The image below features tremolos between notes. The first is between two single notes, and the second is between two chords.

The notation for a tremolo is also used in pitched and unpitched percussion music as a roll. Tomorrow's topic will offer further explanation of instrument specific markings.

In music written for a soloist, the composer will occasionally write or imply a special, ornamented section of the music called the **cadenza.** This passage of music may be improvised or written out and is often played in a liberal style with rhythmic freedom. A cadenza is an opportunity for virtuosic display of technique and musicianship.

Day 21 - Instrument Specific Markings

Throughout this week, the markings, symbols, and terms studied have been applicable to large instrument groupings, if not all instruments in some instances. Because there are a multitude of instruments that are each uniquely designed with distinctive sounds, there are markings that are used to instruct musical effects or alterations that only particular instruments can do. On this final day of this guide, we will study the most significant of these specific markings.

Perhaps the most popularly played instrument worldwide, we must mention the piano and its pedal. Piano and keyboard feature pedals that are used to change to tones being played in some way. Which pedal and how often to use it are usually marked in the music using symbols and brackets.

If a complete set, a piano or keyboard will have three pedals to use. On the far right is the most important pedal, the **damper pedal.** If a digital keyboard only has one pedal, it will be this one. When a note is played with the damper pedal depressed, that note and any subsequent notes played while the pedal is down will be sustained until the sound of the strings naturally decays or the pedal is released. The damper pedal is often called the sustain pedal because of this. The damper pedal functions to either lengthen notes so that large leaps between notes will be smooth, or to richen the tone of notes and chords. The original markings that indicate to push or release the pedal are below. On the left, Ped. abbreviates pedal, and indicates to depress the pedal. The flowery dot indicates when to release the pedal.

There are also brackets with points used to notate the depressing and releasing of the damper pedal. The first bracket below would be found under the measure or system it applies to, and can be shorter or longer than a single measure. The far left, vertical line would be the moment to press the pedal. The pedal is held down for the duration of the line, and released at the far-right vertical line. These brackets can be used alone or repeatedly.

The bracket above has small triangles that indicate to release and then immediately depress the damper pedal at that moment in the music. It is a quick movement used to clear and reset the pedal

Sometimes, a piece will only indicate "pedal throughout" and leave it to the performer to decide where pedaling is appropriate. It is assumed to use the damper pedal if not specified.

The leftmost pedal of the three on a full piano set is the **una corda.** It is oftentimes called the soft pedal because when depressed, the una corda pedal shifts the inner action of the piano in a way that results in a softer sound when notes are played. Use of this pedal will be indicated with the word phrase "una corda", until the words "tre corde" appear, implying "one string" to "three strings".

The middle pedal is the least used of the three. The **sostenuto pedal** sustains only the notes that are being played when the pedal is depressed, and does not affect any notes afterward. Its use is indicated in music using either the abbreviation "S.P." or "Sost."

Arguably, the second most popular instrument worldwide might be the guitar. Instruments in the guitar family share some markings and symbols with the orchestral string family, but they take on a unique approach and definition depending on the instrument. For example, the two symbols below on guitar mean either **downstroke** or **upstroke**, which indicates the direction of the pick, finger, or strum hand.

The same exact markings are used in orchestral string music to indicate bow directions, **up bow** and **down bow**, so it is rather similar in meaning. The downbow or down stroke symbol is the squarish marking, and the upbow or upstroke is the triangular marking in the image above.

Because string **bends**, **hammer-ons**, **pull-offs**, and **slides** are all features of the guitar family of instruments, there are markings specific to each one. These are printed and labeled below.

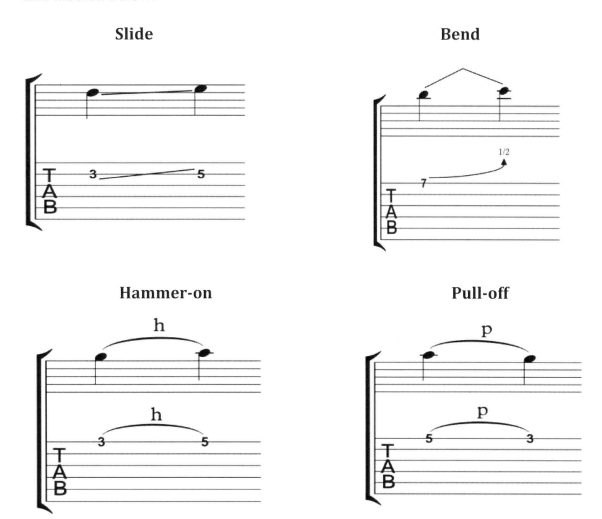

A string bend is notated with a pointed line on the staff and as a curved line on tablature. The number at the end of the arrow directs how far to bend the string. In the example of a bend on the far left, the "½" indicates to bend the string up a half step. The staff represents this with the notes B to C, a half step. Hammer-ons are notated with a slur and the letter "h, and pull-offs are notated with a slur and the letter "p". A slide looks similar to a glissando, which on guitar, basically is a glissando.

Because they use a bow primarily, orchestral string music often has bow specified directions notated. Aside from down bow and up bow marks, **pizzicato** is seen frequently. Pizzicato is a style of plucked playing without the bow. To resume bowing, the music will be marked with the word **arco**, Italian for bow.

In music written for instruments that use air, such as the voice, woodwinds, or brass instruments, **breath marks** may be included to direct the musician to the proper places to **phrase**. A phrase in music is like a musical sentence that should flow as one entity and not be interrupted by a pause unless a rest is indicated. Editors and composers will occasionally specify the desired location to breath using an apostrophe above the staff.

Breath Mark

,

Yesterday we viewed several examples of how a glissando can be notated. There are a few instruments that can do a special and similar type of sliding sound that is called a **portamento.** With a glissando, technically the notes are ascending or descending chromatically, or in half steps, from the initial to final note between the marked line. Instruments like the violin or voice are capable of sliding their sound in at every possible frequency between half steps even. In a glissando, the half steps are discernable, whereas in a portamento, no discrete steps are identifiable. Because the portamento is often notated using the same type of line as a glissando, there exists much debate about its use. Performance practice and the intended instrument's capabilities are to be considered when discerning between a glissando or portamento.

Suggested listening for portamento:

Jazz – "Rhapsody in Blue" by George Gershwin

In the percussion family of instruments, rolls and diddles are a technique and sound specific to drums, mallet percussion, and other accessory percussion. Rolls are notated the same way tremolos are. The two slashes below the whole note in the first measure indicate to roll at a sixteenth-note pace. One slash would be eighth notes, and beyond two slashes goes into further divisions of the sixteenth note.

An additional marking you may come across depending on the instrument you play the word "mute". Mute can hold various meanings depending on the instrument. Most commonly, the word is referring to a device called a mute that can be attached to some instruments in the string and brass families of instruments. Mutes change the tone of the sound, the volume, or both. In guitar, the marking "palm mute", abbreviated "P.M." is commonly used to indicate for the player to lay their palm of their strum hand on the strings to dampen the sound.

Week 3 Highlights

- Music comes to life when expression is added. Composers use terms and symbols to guide expression.
- The standard language for expressive terms is Italian.
- Dynamics are the expressive indications of loudness and softness in music.
- Common dynamic markings are *pp, p, mp, mf, f,* and *ff.*
- Articulation markings assist musicians on how to approach a note or group of notes. These add to the stylistic interpretation of the music.
- Common articulation markings are the slur, tenuto, staccato, accent, and marcato.
- The mood of the music can also be reflected with expressive text, such as *dolce* or *agitato.*
- Tempo markings are sometimes indicated using Italian terms rather than a BPM setting. The most common of these are largo, adagio, andante, moderato, allegro, and presto. Italian suffixes can be used to expand these tempo markings, and additional words are also used.
- There are several markings that indicate gradual changes in tempo, such as *ritardando, rallentando,* and *accelerando.*
- Fermatas hold out a note for an unspecified duration. A caesura pauses the music for a moment, like an extended rest.
- All of these markings are relative to each other, the character and time period of the piece, and the interpretation of the performer.
- Volta brackets are endings of varying musical content used for repeated sections of music.
- There are repeat structures that use da capo, dal segno, fine, and codas to indicate jumps and repeats.
- Ornaments such as the trill, mordent, turn, or grace note are used to embellish the music.
- There are dozens of instrument specific markings that are commonly seen in music for that instrument, such as bow markings or breath marks.

Afterword

Hats off to your completion of the entire "How to Read Music for Any Instrument: Daily Exercises to Understand Music in 21 Days." Comprehension of the elements of rhythm, pitch, and expression studied over the last twenty-one days will contribute immensely to your growth as a musician. Take the knowledge and skills acquired through these studies and apply them through regular practice on your instrument or instruments of choice. If you are able, study with a private teacher to expedite your musical mastery.

Should you wish to expand your musical knowledge beyond the content of this guide, the study of music theory and music composition analyze the more advanced complexities of the subject. Upon completion of this guide, you are well-equipped to continue your journey along the path to musical literacy and applying it to your chosen instrument. I am confident that the experience you've gained over these last three weeks will serve as a foundation to build upon as you pursue your future musical endeavors.

You are encouraged to use this guide as a reference tool whenever you may need to reacquaint yourself with a term or symbol. Perhaps you may even re-read it on occasion for a quick refresher. The following pages include all of the terms and symbols analyzed throughout the guide with page numbers and a brief description for quick reference.

Glossary of Terms and Symbols

Term	Definition	Symbol	Page
Acciaccatura	a grace note meant to be played very quickly either immediately on or before the beat, the placement varies		123
Accidentals	flats, sharps and naturals are collectively referred to as "accidentals"		68
Ad Libitum	translates to "with free rhythm and expression"; this gives the performer freedom with the marked portions of said music	ad lib.	102
Agitato	translates to "agitated"; this implies to player more loudly, and sometimes quicken the tempo, or speed		102
All' Ottava	"at the octave" this abbreviates to play the designated music up an octave if the symbol is located above the staff, or down the octave if the symbol is located below the staff. See also, ottava bassa	8va	73
Allegro	translates to "cheerful"; in music, it is described as "bright, brisk, or fast tempo"(120-156 BPM)		104
Alto Clef	a C clef that indicates Middle C (C4) is on line three of the staff		60
Anacrusis or pick-up note	a note or sequence of notes that occur before the first complete measure or bar		26
Andante	translates to "walking"; often described as a "walking pace"(76-108 BPM)		103
Andantino	an ambiguous term, it is currently interpreted as "a litter faster than andante"(80-108 BPM)		105
Appoggiatura	a grace note that, unlike the Acciaccatura, receives half the value of the principal note		124
Arco	translates to "bow"; this implies that one should resume bowing at this point in the music		128
Articulation	how a note is attacked or approached in performance		98
Backbeat	A style of music that only emphasizes the weak beats of the measure		36
Bar	another term for measure, a segment of time in music.		7
Bar Line	the vertical line used in a musical score to mark a division between bars		7
Bass Clef/F Clef	the clef used for instruments with low to middle ranges in pitch. Designates line four of the staff as where to place the pitch F3 by the placement of the two vertical dots around that line	𝄢	57
Beam	line used to group eighth notes together		16
Beat	the beat is the audible conception of the pulse, in respect to the time signature		4
Beats Per Minute	the pace of the song, measured by the number of beats occurring in sixty seconds	BPM	5
Bend	a stylistic marking used in music for the guitar family		128
Breath Mark	may be included to direct the musician to the proper places to phrase		128
Cadenza	a special section of music that may be written out or improvised by the player, to display their musicianship and technique		125
Caesura	directs the performer or ensemble to completely stop, as if the music were paused	//	107
Cantabile	translates to "singable, songlike"; usually implies that the music should be performed in smooth, lyrical manner		102
Chord	whenever two notes occur simultaneously		87
Chord Inversion	when the notes of a triad are arranged in a different order on the staff, using the same three notes		88
Chord Symbol	Capital letter used to label or indicate a chord in music		89
Chromatic Scale	a twelve note sequences consisting of half-steps only, that extends an octave		78
Circle of Fifths	lists the keys using the interval of a fifth to progress to the next key signature, starting with C major/A minor		83

Common Time	4/4 time, the most commonly used time signature	C	8
Composer	one who writes music		4
Compound Meter	a meter whose beat is divisible into three divisions		31
Crescendo	A gradual change in volume that increases over time		95
Cut-time	2/2 time, or a C with a vertical line through it	₵	30
Damper Pedal	functions to either lengthen notes so that large leaps between notes will be smooth, or to richen the tone of notes and chords	Ped.	126
D.C. al Coda	instructs the musician to, at that point in the music, jump to the beginning, play until the coda sign, then jump to the coda.		117
D.C. al Fine	indicates to jump back to the beginning of the song, and play until the fine sign		114
De Capo	directs the musician to start playing "from the beginning". Usually abbreviated to D.C.	D.C	114
Decrescendo	A gradual change in volume that decreases over time		95
Del Segno	also referred to as the D.S., this indicates to jump back to the "Segno" in the music.	D.S.	115
Diminuendo	used interchangeably with decrescendo	dim.	95
Dolce	translates to "sweetly"; this implies that music should be played delicately, likely on the softer side of dynamics		102
Dotted Half Note	a half note with a rhythmic dot, it is worth three beats in most time signatures	𝅗𝅥.	23
Double Bar Line	denotes the end of the song		7
Down Bow	this symbol directs the bow of an orchestral instrument to played downward		127
Downbeat	the first beat of a measure, and the most emphasized strong beat in any time signature.		8
Downstroke	this symbol indicates that the intended strum direction of the player's pick, finger, or strum hand, is downwards		127
D.S. al Coda	instructs the musician to, at that point in the music, jump to the segno, play until the coda sign, then jump to the coda.		117
D.S. al Fine	instructs the musician to jump back to the segno marked in the music, and play from there until the fine		116
Duple Meter	any meter in which the beats are grouped into two		29
Duplet	a tuplet that contains two sounds		43
Dynamics	the loudness or softness of music is organized using these symbols	pp, p, mp, mf, f, ff, cresc. decresc.	94
Eighth notes - Quaver	a note held for one eighth of a whole note	♪	16
Eighth Rest	a rest held for one eighth of a whole note		16
Enharmonic	two notations or spellings for the same note		66
Espressivo	can be interpreted to add loudness and softness for contrast in order to emote throughout the musical line		97
-etto	translates to "little"; used as a suffix with tempo markings		105
Fermata	indicates for that note or chord to be sustained for longer than normal, the duration is up to the performer's interpretation		107
Fine	translates to "end", and means this in music. It is often used in conjunction with either de capo(D.C.), or del segno(D.S.)		114
Flat Sign	indicates that a note is to be played one half step lower	♭	65
Forte	a dynamic marking, forte translates to loud	𝆑	94
Forte-Piano	indicates that you play the first part of the note loud, before immediately dropping to soft	fp	97

130

Term	Definition	Symbol	Page
Half Note - Minim	a note that is half the duration of a whole note		13
Half Rest	a rest held for two beats		14
Half step - Semitone	the shortest distance between two pitches		63
Hammer-on	a stylistic marking found in music for the guitar family	h	128
Harmonic Minor Scale	The natural minor scale with the seventh pitch raised by a half step		78
Harmony	created when tones are combined, and sound simultaneously		87
Hertz	the number of wave cycles made by a sound within one second	Hz	50
Hook/Flag	the "tail" of an eighth note when written as a single beat of sound		16
Interval	the distance between two consecutive or simultaneous notes		69
-issimo	this suffix indicates an exaggeration of the attached tempo		95
Inverted Mordent	like a trill, but much shorter in duration; alternates between the written note, one step above that, and back to original note. Also see mordent		121
Key	a system of functionally related notes derived from the major and minor scales, with a central note, or "home note"		80
Key Signature	notates what the key of the entire song, or section of song, is		80
Larghissimo	the slowest tempo marking possible(24 BPM or less)		105
Largo	translates to "wide, or broad" and indicates a very slow tempo(anywhere from 40-60 BPM)		103
Lead Sheet	this type of music notes the melody on the staff and includes the harmony as chord symbols written above		89
Ledger lines	the shorter lines that create additional lines beyond the staff		59
Legato	translates to "smooth, connected"; this term to the style of music in which the aim is a smooth, connected flowing sound		98
Major Scale	A stepwise arrangement of seven pitches, with the sequence of steps being "Whole-whole-half-whole-whole-whole-half"		75
Marcato	a marking similar to the accent in meaning, but the interpretation is more forceful and loud than an accent		100
Measure	a specific segment of time in the music, separated by vertical bar lines		7
Melody	a musically satisfying sequence of notes that server as the principal part of a piece		87
Meno Mosso	translates to "Less motion"; this marking indicates that the portion selected should be played more slowly than the previous part		105
Meter	indicates the number of beats in a measure, and the value of the beat.		7
Metronome	a device used to mark time at a selected rate with a tick or tone		5
Mezzo	translates to "moderately"; this is a suffix that is used in conjunction with forte or piano	mp, mf	95
Natural Minor Scale	A stepwise arrangement of seven pitches, with the sequence of steps being "Whole-half-whole-whole-half-whole-whole"		78
Moderato	translates to "moderately"; this "moderate" tempo marking sits anywhere from 98-112 BPM		103
Mordent	like a trill, but much shorter in duration; alternates between the written note, one step below that, and back to original note		121
Natural Sign	the sign that cancels any sharp or flat and indicates to play the natural given pitch		67

Ottava Bassa	"below the octave", indicates to play the designated music down an octave from where it appears	*8vb*	73
Pentatonic Scale	a five note sequence that excludes any half steps		79
Percussion Clef	a clef used for unpitched percussion instruments		62
Phrase	a musical sentence that should flow as one entity and not be interrupted by a pause unless a rest is indicated		120
Piano	a dynamic marking, piano translates to soft	*p*	94
Piu	translates to "more"; this is a suffix that is used in conjunction with other markings		95
Pizzicato	a style of plucked playing without the bow	*pizz.*	128
Poco	translates to "little"		96
Poco a Poco	translates to "little by little"; when combined with a dynamic marking, it implies a longer duration of volume change		96
Polyrhythm	a rhythm that makes use of two or more different rhythms at once		45
Portamento	marking that indicates a slide, like glissando, but one without discernible steps		129
Presto	translates to "soon"; in music, presto is a very, very fast tempo(168-200 BPM)		104
Pull-off	A stylistic marking used in music for the guitar family	p	128
Pulse	the steady, constant rate of the perceived beat in music		4
Quadruple meter	any meter in which the beats are grouped into four		29
Quadruplet	a tuplet that contains four sounds		44
Quarter Note - Crotchet	a single note worth a quarter of a whole note		13
Quarter Rest	a rest held for one beat		14
Quintuplet	a tuplet that contains five sounds		45
Rallentando	translates to "slowing down"; this marking is also used to gradually slow tempo	*rall.*	105
Register	numerical classification of pitches of the same letter name, or pitch class		52
Repeat Sign	stipulates that you play a section of music again, or "repeat"		10
Rhythm	the systematic arrangement of musical sounds		8
Rhythmic Dot	a symbol that adds duration of half of the value of the note that it is attached to		23
Ritardando	translates to "delaying"; this marking is used to gradually slow tempo	*rit. or ritard.*	105
Root	the "home note"(or starting note) of a chord; a triad is named after it's root		88
Root Position	refers to how the three notes in a triad are sequenced, the the name of the chord as the bottom pitch		88
Rubato	music marked rubato can be sped up or slowed down nearly at will, you are given time "to rob" just as it's translation implies		108
Scale	any graduated sequence of notes, tones, or intervals dividing an octave		75
Segno	a sign in music used to mark a jump, used with the navigational phrase "Del Segno"	𝄋	115
Septuplet	a tuplet that contains seven sounds		45
Sextuplet	a tuplet that contains six sounds		45

Term	Definition	Symbol	Page
Simple Meter	any meter in which the beats are grouped into two		29
Sixteenth Note - Semiquaver	a note held for one sixteenth of a whole note		17
Sixteenth Rest	a rest held for one sixteenth of a whole note		19
Slide	like a glissando, but for guitar		128
Slur	a curved line connecting pitches of different classes; the notes must be changing, or it is just a tie, not a slur		98
Smorzando	to "smother the dynamic to nothing"	*smorz.*	97
Sostenuto Pedal	sustains only the notes that are being played when the pedal is depressed, and does not affect any notes afterward	sost. or s.p.	127
Staccato	like the tenuto, the staccato appears above or below a note, and indicates for the note to be played "detached"		99
Staff	the five horizontal lines with spaces between them that notes are placed on or between in music		54
Stem	the vertical line that extends from some note heads		13
Straight Eighths	the default state of eighth notes in music - even distribution within the beat		109
Strong Beat	the beat that is stressed in a measure, it is emphasized over the weak beat		8
Subito	translates to "suddenly"; this marking indicates that volume changes are to happen suddenly rather than gradually	*Sub.*	96
Swing Eighths	still a division of a single beat, the two sounds aren't evenly distributed - the first gets more of the beat, making it feel relaxed		109
Syncopation	a rhythmic sequence that temporarily displaces the strong versus weak beat structure in a measure by emphasizing the weak beat		36
Tablature/Tab	instrument-specific notations with their own style of staff used for the guitar family of instruments		62
Tempo	the pace or speed of a musical composition		5
Tempo Marking	marking that indicates the speed of the music		5
Tempo Primo	translates to "first time"; directs you to return to the previous tempo that was marked before the fluctuation, like A Tempo		105
Tenor Clef	a C clef with Middle C (C4) designated to line four of the staff		61
Tenuto	this marking indicates to play the note at its fullest value, creating minimal separation between notes		99
Tie	connects two or more notes, adding their values together		21
Time Signature	the printed notation of meter		7
Treble Clef/G Clef	the clef used for instruments with middle to high ranges of pitch. Designates line two of the staff as the location of the pitch G4, with a circular swirl around the line		55
Tremolo	seen either as a rapid reiteration of a single note, or a rapid alteration of two different notes		125
Triad	implies three notes or tones, sounding simultaneously		88
Trill	alternation between the printed note and the note one higher on the staff in accordance with the key signature	tr or tr~	120
Triple Meter	any meter in which the beats are grouped into three		30
Triplet	a tuplet that contains three sounds		41
Tuplet	any rhythm that is an abnormal division or subdivision of the beat		41
Turn	a symbol that represents multiple note additions; an S shaped symbol, the shape of the curve indicates the directions of the notes		122
Una Corda Pedal	shifts the inner action of the piano in a way that results in a softer sound when the notes are played	*una corda*	127
Unison	when two consecutive notes are of the same pitch		74
Up Bow	this symbol directs the bow of an orchestral instrument to played upward		127

Upbeat	the final beat of a measure, that precedes and anticipates the subsequent downbeat		8
Upstroke	this symbol indicates that the intended strum direction of the player's pick, finger, or strum hand, is upwards	V	127
Volta Brackets	additions that are used when an excerpt of the music is to be played again(repeated) with alternative endings on the repeat		112
Weak Beat	the unstressed beat in a measure, sometimes referred to as the off-beat.		8
Whole Note - Semibreve	a single note held for four beats	o	13
Whole Rest	a rest held for the entirety of a measure		14
Whole step - Tone	the distance of two half steps		63

Answer Key

Exercise 3.9

Exercise 3.10

Exercise 4.4

Exercise 4.5

Exercise 8.2

6. How many letters are used to organize pitch in music?
    a. Seven
7. Including register classification, what letter name would be the note after C1?
    b. D1
8. What letter comes after "G" in the musical alphabet?
    c. "A"
9. What letter comes before "A" in the musical alphabet?
    d. "G"
10. Are D2 and D3 considered to be of the same pitch class?
    e. Yes

Exercise 9.1

Space 2   Line 4   Line 3   Space 1   Line 1   Line 2   Space 3   Line 5   Space 4

Exercise 9.2

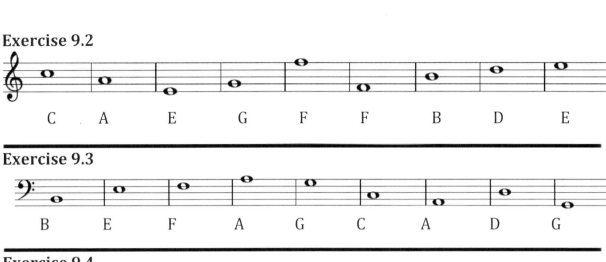

C   A   E   G   F   F   B   D   E

Exercise 9.3

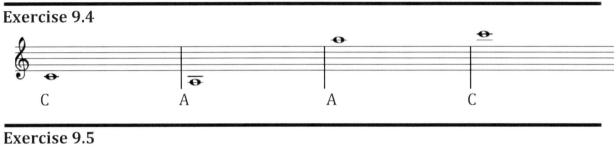

B   E   F   A   G   C   A   D   G

Exercise 9.4

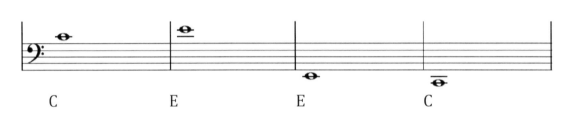

C   A   A   C

Exercise 9.5

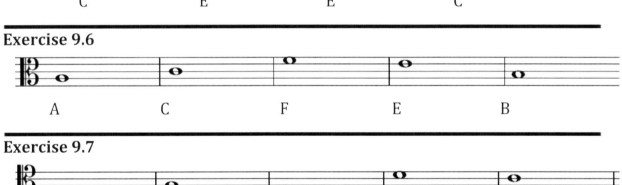

C   E   E   C

Exercise 9.6

A   C   F   E   B

Exercise 9.7

F   A   G   D   C

Exercise 10.3

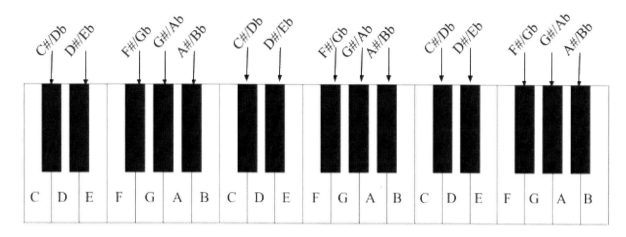

Exercise 10.4

There are five flat notes in the first measure and three sharp notes in the second.

Exercise 10.5

In the first measure, there are two sharp notes and four natural. In the second measure there are two flat notes and three natural.

Exercise 10.6

A to B - whole step up, Db to C - half step down, A to G# - half step down, Bb to C - whole step up, E to F - half step up, D# to E - half step up

Exercise 11.1

2nd   3rd   3rd   2nd   2nd

Exercise 11.2

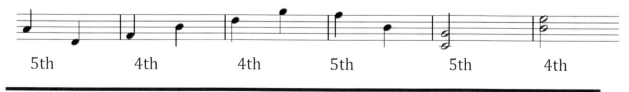

5th   4th   4th   5th   5th   4th

Exercise 11.3

3rd   3rd   7th   5th   5th   3rd   7th

Exercise 11.4

3rd   6th   5th   2nd   3rd   8th   2nd   7th   4th

Exercise 12.1

G A B C D E F# G

Exercise 12.2

D E F G A Bb C D

Exercise 13.1

Gb-Ab-Bb-Cb-Db-Eb-F-Gb/F#-G#-A#-B -C#-D#-E#-F#

Exercise 13.2

F# - G /C# - D/G# - A/D# - E/A# - B/E# - F#

Exercise 13.3

2 flats - Bb/3 flats - Eb/4 flats - Ab/5 flats - Db/6 flats - Gb/7 flats – Cb

Exercise 13.4

D Major=B minor/Ab Major=F minor/F Major=D minor/C Major=A minor/
Db Major=Bb minor/B Major=G# minor

Exercise 14.1

A Major Triad - A, C#, E   C Minor Triad - C, Eb, G
Bb Major Triad - Bb, D, F   D Minor Triad - D, F, A
F Major Triad - F, A, C   F# Minor Triad - F#, A, C#

Exercise 14.2

C = C, E, G   Am= A, C, E   G = G, B, D   F = F, A, C

Exercise 16.1

Slur   Tie   Slur   Slur   Tie

Exercise 16.2

Four duration dots, five staccato dots

Exercise 16.3

Five accent marks, three marcato marks

Exercise 19.1

Measure Order: 1-2-3-4-5-6-7-8-1-2-3-4-5-6-7-9

Exercise 19.2

Measure Order: A-B-C-B-D-E-F-D-E-F-D-E-G-H-H

Exercise 19.3

Fine   D.C. al Fine

Measure Order: A-B-C-D-E-F-G-H-I-J-K-L-A-B-C-D-E-F

Exercise 19.4

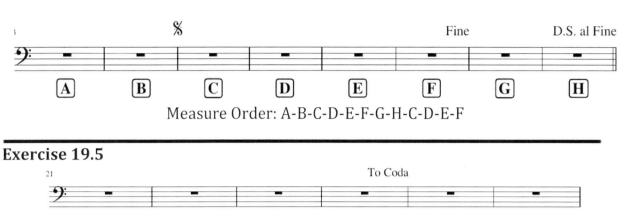

Measure Order: A-B-C-D-E-F-G-H-C-D-E-F

Exercise 19.5

Measure Order: A-B-C-D-E-F-G-H-I-J-A-B-C-D-K-L

Exercise 19.6

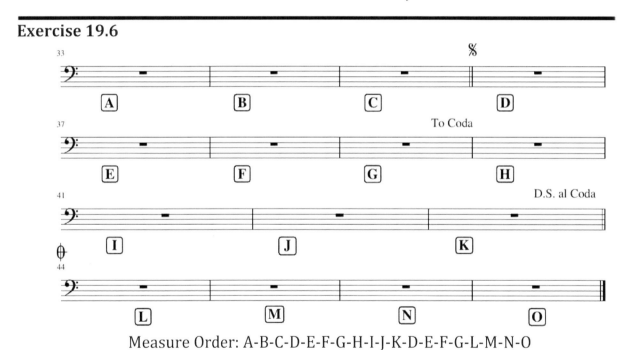

Measure Order: A-B-C-D-E-F-G-H-I-J-K-D-E-F-G-L-M-N-O

Exercise 20.1

D tr E/E tr F#/F# tr G/G tr A/A tr B/B tr C#/C# tr D

Exercise 20.2

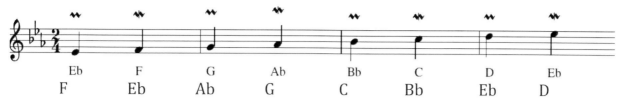

Exercise 20.3

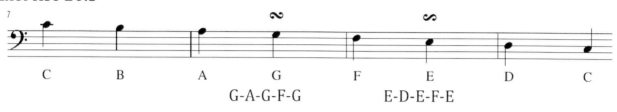

Exercise 20.4

acc. - acciaccatura   app. - appoggiatura

Made in United States
North Haven, CT
02 July 2022

20901257R00080